Sable Angora Rabbit

A PETKEEPER'S GUIDE TO

RABBITS
& GUINEA PIGS

Pink-eyed Golden Guinea Pig

Opal Rex Rabbits – four weeks old

A PETKEEPER'S GUIDE TO

RABBITS
& GUINEA PIGS

**A practical introduction to keeping and
breeding a wide range of these popular pets**

David Alderton

Tetra🖐Press

No. 16054

A Salamander Book

© 1986 Salamander Books Ltd.,
Published in the USA by
Tetra Press,
201 Tabor Road,
Morris Plains,
N.J. 07950

ISBN 3-923880-60-X

Opal Rex Rabbit – adult

Credits

Editor: Geoff Rogers   Design: Stonecastle Graphics
Colour reproductions:
Melbourne Graphics Ltd.
Filmset: SX Composing Ltd.
Printed in Belgium by Henri Proost & Cie, Turnhout.

Author

David Alderton's abiding interest in the field of pet care and natural history began with the study of veterinary medicine at Cambridge University. Now the author of over 20 books, many with a particular emphasis on 'exotic' pets, David still finds time to contribute regularly to general and specialist periodicals in the UK and overseas. In addition to writing, David has always kept and bred a variety of animals and birds, and now runs a highly respected service that offers advice on the needs of animals kept in domestic and commercial environments. Through his consultancy work he has been closely involved in the development of safe non-toxic bedding material for small mammals and is fully conversant with current developments relating to their care.

Consultant

Chris Henwood has kept rodents since his school days and, although he has a wide interest in all forms of animal and plant life, his main interest still lies in this area. He has written several books and articles on the subject of rodents, their care and their genetics. He regularly appears on television and radio programmes as an expert on small animals and has advised a number of programme makers on aspects of rodents and their care. He is a National and International Judge of Hamsters and a founder member of both the Small Mammal Genetics Circle (SMGC) and the National Association of Private Animal Keepers (NAPAK). He maintains a wide collection of animals, including a number of rarely seen rodents and is believed to be one of the few non-zoological collections to have successfully bred the Rock Cavy.

Contents

Introduction

Although both rabbits and guinea pigs have a popular image as children's pets, they do in fact have a much wider appeal. Selective breeding has given rise to a wide variety of different colours and breeds. These have been carefully developed and fostered by groups of dedicated fanciers, and can be seen at the various shows held throughout the world. The exhibition side of keeping rabbits and guinea pigs attracts a very strong following, yet the movement of stock internationally does create problems.

It is usually necessary to quarantine these creatures when moving them from one country to another, because, like other mammals, rabbits and guinea pigs are susceptible to rabies. Partly for this reason, therefore, some breeds have tended to remain localized in their countries of origin, especially in the case of rabbits. If you want to see or even obtain any of the rarer breeds, you will probably need to visit one of the larger shows, where such rabbits

are most likely to be on view and breeders are eager to give advice.

Part of the appeal of rabbits and guinea pigs is their adaptability. They may be kept quite satisfactorily indoors, or, alternatively, they can be housed in outside accommodation throughout the year, provided that they receive adequate protection against the elements, both in summer and winter. The amount of care required does vary somewhat, however, according to the breed concerned. Both long-coated rabbits and guinea pigs are considerably more demanding in terms of their care than shorter haired individuals, and thus are probably best left for the specialist, unless you have a considerable amount of time available to groom your pet on a regular basis. Thankfully, neither rabbits nor guinea pigs are badly affected with breed-related weaknesses, so that generally you can choose either a pure-bred or 'pet' animal without undue worry in either case. Pure-bred animals are no more difficult to keep.

Biology and handling

Rabbits and guinea pigs, although superficially similar, do in fact belong to two separate orders. For many years, however, rabbits were classified with guinea pigs as rodents, since both animals possess prominent incisor teeth and are herbaceous in their feeding habits. Then during the early 20th century, studies revealed a number of significant anatomical and physiological differences between the two and, as a result, rabbits were transferred to a new order, called Lagomorpha.

Rabbits and their relatives

Two families fall within the order Lagomorpha. The family Ochotonidae encompasses the pikas, which lack tails but even so are more reminiscent of mice than rabbits, having short, rounded ears. Rabbits and hares are grouped in the other family, the Leporidae, in which forty-four different species are recognized.

'Lagomorph' means 'hare shaped' and refers to the distinctive physical appearance of these creatures, with their long ears, prominent eyes and powerful hind limbs. The distinction between rabbits and hares tends to reflect a basic difference in lifestyles. Rabbits are usually more sedentary, retreating to a burrow at the onset of danger, whereas hares spend most of their lives above ground, relying on speed to escape predators.

Leporids, as rabbits and hares are collectively known, have a universal distribution, being found on all continents except Antarctica. Among species found in the Arctic tundra is the Arctic Hare (*Lepus timidus*), which is widely spread throughout this northern region, ranging from North America across Europe into Asia. At the onset of winter, this creature undergoes a striking change as its fur lightens from dark brown to white, which helps to conceal it at a time when there is no vegetation to provide natural cover in the environment.

Given the widespread distribution and adaptable nature of leporids, it was inevitable that they would invite human interest. The earliest evidence of this appears in Mayan art, at a time when leporids were also valued as a source of food. Because of its association with humans, the rabbit now has a much wider distribution than originally. The Normans were responsible for introducing rabbits to England, while the early settlers took them to Australia, where they rapidly multiplied into a menace of plague proportions.

Guinea pigs

By contrast, the guinea pig has a very limited distribution, as all fourteen species in the family Caviidae are confined to South America. There is often confusion over the name of these likeable rodents. Called 'cavies' as a result of their generic name *Cavia*, they are also known as guinea pigs, partly because they occur (although not exclusively) in Guiana, a region of northern South America that includes Guyana, Surinam and French Guiana. In addition, they do have a certain physical resemblance to pigs, and cavy meat is said to taste like pork. Indeed, the history of these rodents in captivity stems from the time of the Peruvian Incas,

Above: *A young girl with her pet Netherland Dwarf. Both rabbits and guinea pigs are easy to keep.*

who maintained colonies as a source of food.

The guinea pig is classified as a member of the suborder Caviomorpha, sometimes described as hystricomorph rodents, which also include the porcupines found outside the Americas. These animals can all be distinguished from the main group of rodents, including mice and rats, by the arrangement of their jaw muscles. The masseter muscle of hystricomorphs is divided into two parts, the lateral portion of which is responsible for shutting the jaws. A more significant feature, for the guinea pig breeder, is that the gestation period of these rodents is traditionally much longer than in the mouse-like species of the suborder Myomorpha. The hystricomorph is therefore born in a relatively advanced state of development, with the litter size often smaller as a result. (See pages 86-87.)

Teeth and digestive system
Guinea pigs share with rabbits a basically similar arrangement of teeth, and vitally important to both animals are the sharp incisors at the front of the mouth. These teeth continue growing throughout life and it is essential that the incisors of top and bottom jaws continue to meet correctly. A rabbit's incisors can grow as much as 12.5cm (5in) in a year, but if either tooth is lost or distorted, their sharp cutting edge will be lost and the animal will soon be unable to eat. Deformed incisors can be an inherited weakness in rabbits, so any stock affected in this way should not be used for breeding. However, a rabbit suffering from dental malocclusion, as the condition is known, can be treated by careful cutting back of the teeth at regular intervals. Try to avoid such problems by providing hard items for a rabbit to chew in order to keep its teeth in trim naturally. (See 'Feeding', page 33.)

Guinea pigs lack the small, second pair of incisors found behind the main pair in rabbits, but neither guinea pigs nor rabbits have canine teeth. Instead, behind the incisors,

there is a gap called the diastema. This allows the sides of the cheeks to be drawn in behind the incisors, so that the animal can continue gnawing while regulating what it swallows. Any inedible items can be easily rejected. Behind the diastema are the cheek teeth, first the premolars and then the molars.

The digestive system of rabbits has evolved to ensure that they gain maximum nutritional benefit from their herbaceous diet. Food passes into the stomach, where the digestive process begins, and then progresses through the intestinal tract to the caecum. This closed sac near the junction of the small and large intestines contains active bacteria which help break down cellulose in plant walls so that it can be digested. They also help to synthesize vital vitamins, such as Vitamin B12. Although rabbits can absorb nutrients from the caecum, significant amounts are lost from the body. To remedy this, rabbits consume their own dark, soft caecal pellets as they are voided from the body. These then pass back into the stomach where they mix with fresh food for subsequent digestion.

Refection, as this practice is called, may assist in the digestive process by starting the breakdown of cellulose before the new intake of food reaches the caecum. After this subsequent passage through the intestines, rabbits produce their characteristic dry, hard pellets. Domestic rabbits tend to produce their soft caecal droppings at night, so they may not always be noticed. The rabbit's dependence on bacteria for efficient digestion of foodstuffs has its problems, however, since treatment with antibiotics can have serious effects (see page 37). The guinea pig also has a similar digestive system.

Choosing healthy stock
There are several key points to check before purchasing either a rabbit or a guinea pig, in order to ensure that it is healthy. First, check that the eyes and nose are clear and free from any signs of discharge. This is especially vital in the case of

Rabbit digestive system

Digestive system of a rabbit, showing how the process known as refection, or coprophagy, operates.

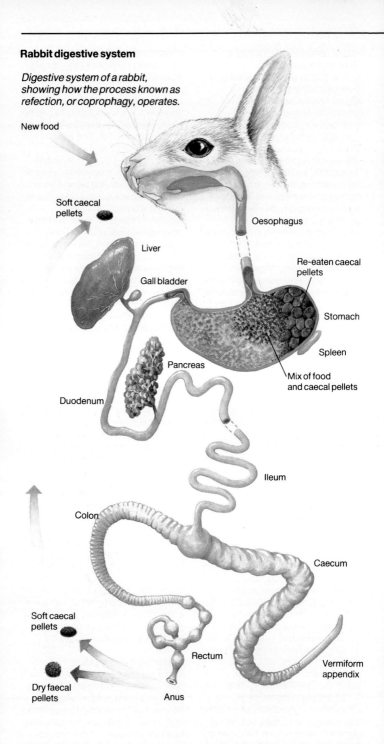

New food

Soft caecal pellets

Oesophagus

Liver

Gall bladder

Re-eaten caecal pellets

Stomach

Spleen

Pancreas

Mix of food and caecal pellets

Duodenum

Ileum

Colon

Caecum

Soft caecal pellets

Rectum

Dry faecal pellets

Anus

Vermiform appendix

Above: *Before buying a rabbit or guinea pig examine its mouth in case the teeth are deformed.*

Above: *Also examine the ear canals of rabbits for the brown scabs of canker caused by mite infestation.*

rabbits, as such symptoms could indicate the serious viral disease myxomatosis or the easily spread bacterial ailment known among breeders as 'snuffles' (see page 37). Indeed, if any of the animals on offer appear to be ailing in this way, it is probably best to look elsewhere.

Check the teeth to ensure that they are aligned correctly, and look at the overall condition of the animal. The coat should be bright and full of lustre, while the backbone ought not to be prominent. Look inside the ears, especially of rabbits, which seem most frequently afflicted with the ear mites that give rise to the flaky, brownish deposits characteristic of canker. Guinea pigs are more prone to parasitic mites and lice, as well as ringworm, all of which can create bald areas. Indeed, any hair loss in guinea pigs should be viewed with suspicion.

Also check the underparts of the animal to ensure that there are no sore patches on the undersides of the legs. This condition, known as hutch burn, is often linked with dirty surroundings. The other point to check is that there is no staining around the vent, nor should it appear abnormally enlarged or distorted, as may occur in older guinea pigs. The nails may be overgrown and need clipping back, but this is not a serious problem.

Sexing
Choosing animals of the right sex can be a vital consideration, especially if you wish to house several guinea pigs together, for

Below: *It is vital to sex guinea pigs accurately, especially if you intend to house a group together. Be sure to examine young stock closely.*

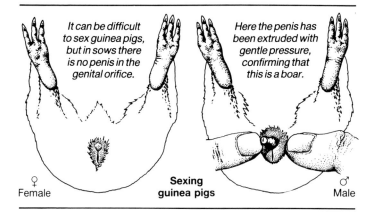

It can be difficult to sex guinea pigs, but in sows there is no penis in the genital orifice.

Here the penis has been extruded with gentle pressure, confirming that this is a boar.

♀
Female

Sexing guinea pigs

♂
Male

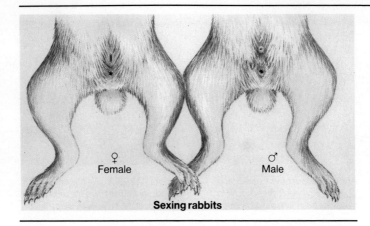

♀
Female

♂
Male

Sexing rabbits

example. Sows (female guinea pigs) can live together quite satisfactorily but boars (males) are likely to fight each other and are best kept apart. With careful handling, it is quite easy to distinguish the sexes, and in mature male guinea pigs, the presence of testes will often be obvious. In young stock especially, however, you will need to make a closer examination of the genital region. To do this, restrain the guinea pig on its back, in the palm of your hand. Using the thumb and finger of the other hand, apply gentle pressure as you move them apart to stretch the skin close to the genital opening. This will bring the penis of the boar into view. In sows there is a membrane covering the vaginal opening. You can see this on close inspection of the genital area, forming a slightly inverted crease.

A similar technique can be used to sex rabbits, with the animal restrained on its back and its hind legs directed forward. It can be difficult to separate the sexes reliably in rabbits under five months of age, although once mature, the buck (male) will be easy to distinguish by its testes. The doe's vulva is narrow, and closer to the anal opening than the penis of the buck. Other physical differences such as head shape may also help to distinguish the sexes, but these are not always a reliable guide.

It is probably best to keep rabbits apart. Two does may live in apparent harmony, and then one

Above: *Sexing rabbits. The scrotal sacs of the male are clearly visible as slight swellings at either side of the vent, as shown here.*

may suddenly start to persecute its companion. Bucks certainly must be housed individually. They can inflict serious damage on each other if they fight, which is almost inevitable in the confines of a hutch.

Handling
Both guinea pigs and rabbits are rarely aggressive towards people, which makes them ideal pets for children. Furthermore, they can live together quite satisfactorily, providing that their accommodation is suitably large. Whereas guinea pigs are quite uniform in size, rabbits tend to be more variable, and it is best to opt for one of the smaller breeds, such as a Netherland Dwarf, as a companion for a guinea pig. Both animals can be kept either indoors or outside.

If you intend to keep a rabbit and guinea pig together, try to introduce them at an early age. Female rabbits may prove more suitable because they are generally less aggressive than bucks.

Handling is relatively straightforward, since neither animal will bite as a general rule. Guinea pigs are especially nimble, however, so ensure that they cannot escape, for example, when their cage door is opened. Try to direct the guinea pig into a corner where you can use one hand to catch and restrain it. Then lift it out with your other hand, taking care to provide additional support beneath. Never leave the guinea pig's hindquarters unsupported: apart from being uncomfortable, it will cause the animal to struggle unnecessarily.

Small rabbits can be handled like guinea pigs, with one hand used to support the body. Never take hold of the rabbit by its long ears, however, leaving the body dangling. Instead, you may use the ears gently to restrain the animal, while holding its body with the other hand. A frightened rabbit will almost

certainly scratch as it kicks out with its powerful hindlimbs, and its claws can cause bleeding.

It is preferable to buy a young rabbit or guinea pig, since if handled regularly from an early age, it will become accustomed to being picked up and will not resent it. An older animal not used to being handled is much less likely to tame well. Another factor to consider is that if the animal's age is unknown, it could even be nearing the end of its natural lifespan.

Breeding for shows

If you have an exhibition rabbit, however, it will almost certainly have a special band applied to the hind leg carrying details of its age. Both rabbits and guinea pigs are exhibited, and if you are interested in showing your animals, it will be best to visit a few breeders first to find the most suitable stock. There can be considerable differences in appearance between pet and exhibition animals, as the latter are bred specifically to conform as closely as possible to prescribed standards laid down by the society concerned.

As a starting point towards setting up a stud of exhibition rabbits or guinea pigs, try to visit as many shows as possible, so you become familiar with the strengths and weaknesses of the stock on display. Unlike some areas of livestock fancying, the cost of such stock is not excessive, compared with average pet animals. There are many clubs catering for those interested in exhibiting both rabbits and guinea pigs, and these provide a useful source of contact when seeking stock. Most established breeders will be keen to help a novice get started in the hobby.

Above left: *Solid rather than cardboard containers are best for transporting rabbits. Those shown are useful for show stock.*

Left: *Always handle rabbits with particular care as they are rather prone to back problems. Indeed, a fatal injury could follow a fall.*

Accommodation

Rabbits and guinea pigs are quite hardy creatures, and can be kept outside for most of the year provided that their quarters are dry and draughtproof. While there are various ways of housing these animals, a hutch of some kind is the most popular option.

Suitable hutches

The typical hutch is made of wood, and constructed in the shape of a box. Ready-built hutches are available from pet stores, but bear in mind that the cheapest design is not likely to be the most satisfactory.

Although a single guinea pig can live in a smaller enclosure than a rabbit, the minimum dimensions should be at least 60cm (24in) long, 45cm (18in) wide (front to back) and 30cm (12in) high. If the accommodation is to house more than one guinea pig, increase the space accordingly, allowing about an extra 930 sq cm (1 sq ft) for each individual.

A rabbit hutch needs to be bigger in all respects; about 90cm (36in) long, 60cm (24in) wide and 60cm (24in) high. Some of the bigger breeds will need an even larger hutch and certainly, if you decide to build the hutch yourself, it is worth designing a relatively large structure which offers the animals plenty of space for exercise. Although they can be let out into a run now and then, this will be no substitute for a large hutch.

Building a hutch

The materials required for building a hutch will depend partly on its ultimate position. If it is to stay indoors, then a less substantial structure is needed. However, avoid using hardboard to construct the shell of the unit, because rabbits especially are likely to gnaw the walls of their enclosure. Hardboard, although relatively inexpensive, is easily destroyed in this way; it can also act rather like a sponge in absorbing urine or water, causing the material to become soggy and warped, and ultimately break up.

Plywood is a more satisfactory alternative, although again, this can also warp over a period of time. Choose 12mm (0.5in) ply, which is less likely to become distorted than thinner sheets. In order to give additional strength to the finished structure, screw the plywood to a basic framework of 2.5cm square (1in square) wood, so that at a later date a panel can be easily removed and replaced if damaged. It is also possible to combine one module of this type with another to create a larger hutch.

A more expensive material to use in place of plywood is tongued-and-grooved wood. Being robust, this creates a snug interior within the finished hutch, leaving no gaps for draughts to penetrate between the boards. The same material can also be used for the roof, although marine plywood covered with roofing felt will form a more durable

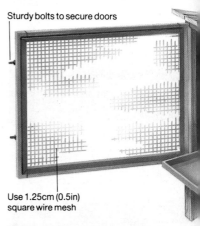

Sturdy bolts to secure doors

Use 1.25cm (0.5in) square wire mesh

This illustration shows the various design features that should be incorporated into a hutch housing either rabbits or guinea pigs. It is not too difficult to construct a hutch yourself, but do ensure that it is large enough. If the hutch is to be kept out of doors, make sure that the occupants are adequately protected from the elements. Since rabbits, especially, will chew woodwork, avoid using wood preservatives within the hutch itself. Choose a level site to ensure that the hutch is stable.

alternative and provide an easy surface for rain to run off. Tongued-and-grooved wood used for the roof may create ledges in which water can accumulate and cause damage.

In order for rain to run off the roof, slope it down to the back of the hutch, which is where the minimum height measurement will apply. Also arrange for the roof to form an overhang at the front, so that water cannot drip directly down on to the entrance and dampen the bedding.

To save it being soaked from below, support the hutch on legs at least 23cm (9in) high. Use wood which is 5cm (2in) square for the supporting legs, preferably incorporating them into the design of the hutch, so that they are more stable. Alternatively, mount the hutch on a course of bricks built up to a similar minimum height.

The basic design

When designing the hutch, be sure to divide it into two parts: an outside area and slightly smaller sleeping quarters, where the animals can retreat at night. A solid partition, with a sliding door set in runners, offers good protection against cold weather, and ensures that the hutch can be cleaned out while the occupants are safely confined in one section or the other as necessary.(This design feature is not always available in purchased hutches.)

The two external doors to the night and day quarters are a vital consideration in the design of a good hutch. They must be strong and preferably secured with bolts to prevent them from falling open inadvertently, thereby allowing the occupants to escape. Another

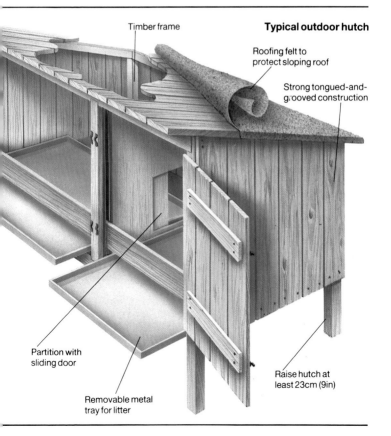

Timber frame

Typical outdoor hutch

Roofing felt to protect sloping roof

Strong tongued-and-grooved construction

Partition with sliding door

Removable metal tray for litter

Raise hutch at least 23cm (9in)

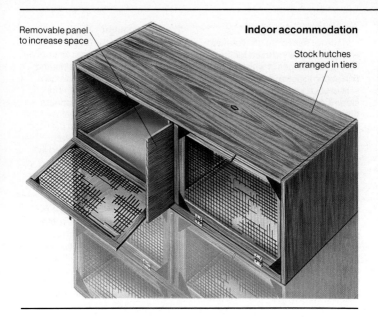

Removable panel to increase space

Indoor accommodation

Stock hutches arranged in tiers

Above: *A stack of hutches for indoor use, such as in a shed. Note the removable centre partitions for maximum flexibility. Hutches of this type are straightforward to build.*

consideration is that many urban areas are now home to colonies of foxes, which are quite capable of opening a simple catch on a cage to get at the animals within.

While the external door to the sleeping quarters can be made of plywood or tongued-and-grooved wood, the adjoining external door to the open area requires a wire mesh cladding on the framework, since it usually forms the front 'viewing' panel of the hutch. Galvanized netting for this purpose should have wire at least 19 gauge (19G) in thickness, as rabbits in particular may chew through finer wire mesh, while foxes can easily get in from outside. The mesh itself must also be small enough to exclude mice, as well as rats, which would also harm the hutch's occupants. Mesh which is 1.25cm (0.5in) square will successfully keep out such vermin. You can buy the necessary short lengths of wire mesh from hardware stores or even garden centres, but it will be cheaper to purchase a roll.

(The surplus can be used to construct an outside run which can be moved around a lawn, allowing the rabbits and guinea pigs to graze outdoors in fine weather.)

Both external doors should be hinged to open outwards. Some owners prefer to hinge the doors at the sides of the hutch; others like the cage doors to open downwards, with hinges at the bottom. The second option is safer, for while you can see the rabbit or guinea pig through the wire mesh when opening the door to the open area, you cannot see into the sleeping quarters. There is always the risk with a side-hinged door that the creature could be sitting up against it and might fall out if it is opened unexpectedly. Whichever design you choose, however, ensure that the hinges, and indeed all fitments, are galvanized to prevent premature rusting. Applying a coat of lubricating oil regularly should also lengthen their lifespan.

Protecting the woodwork
The external parts of the hutch or run can be painted or treated with a wood preservative, but it is probably best not to treat any woodwork which may be chewed by the

animals. Treatment will help to increase the lifespan of the external structure, apart from making it look more attractive. As an additional precaution against the weather, you can apply a double layer of roofing felt not only to the roof, but also to the back and sides of the hutch. Fix this in place with appropriate nails, but ensure that they do not penetrate the hutch itself, where they could injure the animals. You could also fix a low plastic screen across the front of the door to the day quarters. Then if a food pot is tipped over, the contents will remain within the hutch, rather than spilling outside where they are more likely to attract vermin.

Set the hutch in a sheltered position, out of the direction of prevailing winds. In such a place it may well be possible to leave the animals outside throughout the year, although there are circumstances where indoor accommodation is preferable.

Below: *Part of an exhibition breeder's accommodation showing guinea pigs housed in a shed. To save space, the hutches are arranged in blocks at three levels.*

Indoor accommodation

If space outside is limited, rabbits and guinea pigs can be kept indoors permanently. Indeed, some attractive cages are now being marketed for this purpose, although the traditional hutch is also quite satisfactory indoors. If it is to remain indoors there is no need to weatherproof the hutch, although a coat of a safe non-toxic paint will improve its external appearance.

Many exhibition breeders, who keep relatively large stocks, house at least part of their stud in hutches in a suitable outbuilding, typically a converted garden shed. The cages can be arranged in tiers, or it may be preferable to construct the hutches in blocks, usually up to three cages in height. The construction principles are basically the same as for individual units, but the sides of the structure are built as a block, with the floors fitted in. The obvious disadvantage is that the cages cannot be separated, which restricts flexibility.

If a shed is used for shelter, then part of the floor area can be given over to a run which, for guinea pigs in particular, need only be high enough to stop them climbing out.

Rabbits, and especially hares, have a higher reach, so that a roof may be necessary for their run. If the indoor run is positioned at the corner of the shed, then it will require two sides only, but neither cage nor run should be positioned directly in front of a window. It is vital to ensure that sunlight does not cause the temperature inside the run or the shed to rise to fatal levels for the animals.

To provide adequate ventilation in warm weather, ensure that the shed windows are wide opening or removable, with a covering of wire mesh mounted in the open space. Similarly, incorporate a false wire mesh door into the structure so that the main door can be left open, without fear of other animals gaining access to the stock housed inside the shed.

It can be particularly dangerous to use a conservatory for housing rabbits or guinea pigs, since the large area of glass can cause the temperature inside to rise very rapidly on hot days. Painting the glass white or using sunblinds may alleviate this problem to some extent, but good ventilation is also vital in such situations.

Heating and ionizers There is usually no need to provide heating in a garden shed during the colder months of the year, although a light may be useful when feeding the animals on dark winter days.

Below: *An ionizer in action. This electrical device is highly recommended to reduce levels of dust and infectious agents in the air.*

Nevertheless, it may be worthwhile insulating the shed with either polystyrene or fibreglass insulation quilt boarded behind plywood or hardboard, which can then be painted as desired. This layer of insulation will help to lower the temperature slightly in summer as well as keep the interior warmer in winter. If heating is required, use electric greenhouse tubular heaters, which can be set under thermostatic control. Ensure that all external electrical wiring is carried out by a competent electrician, and that it conforms to the necessary safety standards. Beware particularly of using paraffin (kerosene) heaters, which are especially dangerous in an environment where animals and highly combustible materials are found together.

One piece of equipment that can be particularly valuable indoors is an ionizer, which will reduce the amount of dust in the atmosphere. Over a period of time, some people develop an allergy to hay, and an ionizer will minimize this risk. Ionizers can also help to prevent the spread of disease, since microorganisms will also be precipitated from the air by acquiring negative charges. (Basically, an ionizer produces a stream of negatively charged ions that cling to dust and other airborne particles and cause them to precipitate out on to earthed surfaces, which are positively charged by comparison.)

Although ionizers are normally operated off a mains electricity supply, battery-operated models

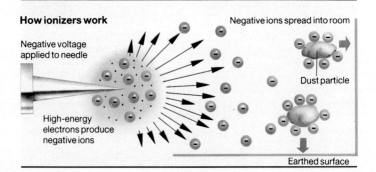

How ionizers work

Negative voltage applied to needle

High-energy electrons produce negative ions

Negative ions spread into room

Dust particle

Earthed surface

are also available and can be especially useful in a shed. The equipment will not harm the animals in any way, is inexpensive to operate, quite durable and does not require sophisticated maintenance. If it is difficult to find a local supplier, look in one of the birdkeeping journals, where ionizers are most frequently advertised.

Discouraging vermin If you keep a number of rabbits or guinea pigs in a particular area, it is almost certain that mice, or even rats, will be attracted to it. Although ultrasonic rodent scarers are now available, these are likely to prove equally disturbing to the legitimate occupants of the shed, which will be unable to escape the high-pitched, distressing sounds produced by such machines. It is probably best, therefore, to use one of the traps that catch vermin alive, rather than opting for a killer trap which will also maim any rabbit or guinea pig that escapes from its cage and sets off the trap.

Do make every effort to dispose of unwelcome rodents as soon as possible. Apart from disturbing stock, and possibly causing cannibalism of offspring in rabbits, such vermin may also introduce serious diseases such as yersiniosis (pseudotuberculosis). If in doubt, call in a professional pest-control group to eliminate the vermin. This can prove the most effective method, and avoids placing poison in any position where your own animals could come into contact with it.

Good hygiene is also valuable in minimizing the risk of attracting such pests to the site. Sweep up any spilt foodstuffs, especially cereals such as crushed oats, every day, even if wire-floored cages are being used. A solid concrete floor to the shed will act as a partial deterrent to rodents, while using 1.25cm (0.5in) square mesh on door and window covers also impedes their access.

Litter and bedding
A rabbit or guinea pig will need suitable bedding in its hutch,

especially if it is living out of doors. Equip the hutch with two removable trays which fit within the two compartments of the cage. They should cover the whole of the interior, and ideally be made of sheet metal, although with no sharp or loose ends on which the animals could injure themselves or catch their toes. The trays can then easily be removed and emptied out when the doors are opened. You will need to make these trays since they are not usually available in ready-built hutches.

What are the options for lining or bedding material? Here, we review the most common types available.

Sawdust Sawdust is the traditional litter used to line cages and hutches, but do ensure that the wood it comes from has not been treated with harmful chemicals. If ingested by accident, such chemically treated sawdust could kill your pet. This can happen quite easily if damp greenfood, for example, is placed on the bedding, as sawdust will adhere readily to it. Softwood sawdust, which is whitish, is preferable to darker types because it is coarser and therefore more absorbent.

Wood shavings The other lining to consider for the hutch floor is wood shavings. These tend to be less dusty than sawdust, but you may need a relatively larger quantity to cover the same area effectively. One advantage of shavings is that they adhere less readily to foodstuffs than sawdust. They are also less likely to irritate the nose of a rabbit, for example, and to cause the eye problems which are most often encountered in the various red-eyed breeds.

Straw and hay Straw and hay are both used as bedding materials, but hay also provides good food for the animals. Since it is more costly than straw, some owners prefer to offer only limited amounts of hay, particularly during the warmer months of the year when the quality of bedding is less significant.

Above: *Various popular types of bedding materials used for rabbits and guinea pigs. Top row from the left: straw, hay, paper bedding. Shavings and sawdust are below.*

Although oat straw may be eaten, its nutritive value is well below that of hay and, as it contains numerous tough stalks, it is also more likely than hay to damage an animal's eyes. Wheat and barley straw are also best avoided for this reason and because they are less likely to be eaten.

Before buying hay or straw, always look at a sample to ensure that it is clean, and neither mouldy not excessively dusty. Good quality meadow hay is recommended, for it contains a variety of other plants, such as clover, as well as grass. With just a few rabbits or guinea pigs, the cost of providing hay rather than straw is minimal. Indeed, although you can buy all bedding materials in small quantities, it is much more economical to buy a relatively large amount, such as a bale of hay, at one time. Keep it in dry surroundings until it is needed. Although you will probably have to replenish the hay day by day as it is eaten, avoid overcrowding the hutch with bedding, particularly when the weather is mild.

Paper bedding Paper bedding, marketed for various small rodents, is an alternative to be considered. It is available in two forms: granulated or shredded. As there is very little dust associated with these products, they can be especially useful in the home. Most brands are checked to ensure that they contain no toxic chemicals, and will therefore be harmless if eaten. The highly absorbent granulated form can be used in place of sawdust or shavings, while the shredded type makes a snug bed.

Cleaning
The hutch will need cleaning out at least once a week, and probably more frequently, depending on the number of animals it houses and whether they spend much of the day in an outside run. Cleanliness is particularly vital during warm weather to minimize the risk of attracting flies, which may lay their eggs close to the soiled area of the cage and can cause the condition described as 'fly strike' (see page 44 of the 'Health care' section).

Rabbits, in particular, tend to use one spot in the hutch as a toilet, and have been trained to use a cat litter tray quite successfully in the home. You may be able to devise a similar system in the hutch, emptying the contents of the tray daily. The soiled litter can make a useful addition to the compost heap if you have one, so avoiding the need to dispose of a relatively large quantity of litter by more conventional means, such as with the household refuse.

Various pieces of household equipment will ease the cleaning process. A paint scraper, for example, can be used to remove damp sawdust from the tray, while a dustpan and brush is useful for sweeping the base of the hutch. If the litter is to be moved to another part of the garden, then empty the trays directly into a wheelbarrow. This will be much easier than trying to guide the debris into the narrow opening of a plastic sack. Once you have cleaned one side of the hutch, move the occupant through to the other side and close the intervening door while you clean the other side.

You may need to scrub the hutch out from time to time; do this only when the weather is warm, so that the interior will dry thoroughly before the quarters are reoccupied.

Building an outdoor run
Animals kept inside will certainly appreciate being allowed to run about freely in an enclosed area of garden, but there is always the risk that they might nibble valued plants, or, alternatively, poisonous ones. Guinea pigs especially are vulnerable to attacks by cats, while dogs can be attracted to rabbits

roaming free in a garden without supervision. It can also prove difficult to catch a rabbit or guinea pig at liberty in a large area, so overall it seems preferable to provide them with a spacious run for outdoor exercise.

A simple rectangular run can be constructed using a mesh-covered framework of 2.5cm (1in) square wood. Ideally, make this in individual sections and then join them together. In order to protect the woodwork, extend the covering mesh on to the adjacent face of the framework. When assembled, the wood will then be entirely covered with mesh, and all cut ends of wire out of reach of the animals within. Alternatively, trim the sharp ends back as close as possible and then tack battening over them to ensure that they cannot injure the animals. A loose piece of wire could blind a rabbit, for example, and it is vital to eliminate all such dangers from their quarters, whether inside or outside.

The height of the run should correspond to the recommended height for the hutch. It is best to design the 'roof' panel to fit inside

Below: *A typical outdoor run. Ensure that the bottom is wired over and that the roof can be adequately secured in position by strong bolts or clasps to deter likely predators.*

Outdoor run

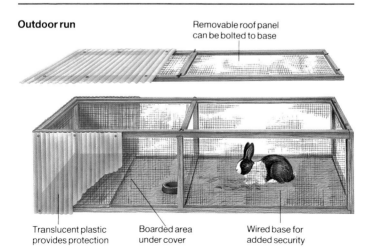

Removable roof panel
can be bolted to base

Translucent plastic
provides protection

Boarded area
under cover

Wired base for
added security

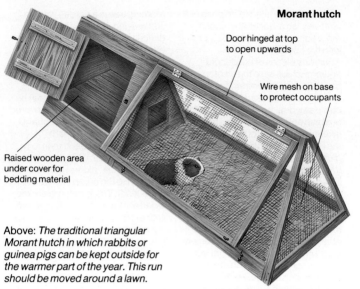

Morant hutch

Door hinged at top to open upwards

Wire mesh on base to protect occupants

Raised wooden area under cover for bedding material

Above: *The traditional triangular Morant hutch in which rabbits or guinea pigs can be kept outside for the warmer part of the year. This run should be moved around a lawn.*

the sides of the structure, resting flush with the top of the unit and supported by a batten of 2.5cm (1in) wood set at an appropriate height beneath. It can be hinged in place, and held with a hasp and padlock, although this can prove rather cumbersome. As an alternative, fix the roof panel to the frame using small bolts. You can then lift out the entire panel without difficulty, while ensuring that the occupants are safe within the confines of the run.

Cover one end of the run on the sides and top with transluscent plastic sheeting to afford some protection against a torrential thunderstorm, for example, while the animals are in the run. Wire over the floor as well so that the occupants cannot be harmed even if a dog manages to get underneath.

Your run can be designed in other ways. The so-called Morant hutch is a traditional alternative, built to a triangular design and featuring an apexed roof. In this instance, cladding forms the shelter at one end, where there is often a raised wooden area on the floor for bedding to be placed. However, catching the animals is likely to be more difficult in a run of this type, especially with more than one in the enclosure. Since one of the sides

Siting hutch/run

1 Site hutch near a path for access.
2 Move the run in sequence around an area of lawn so as not to damage the grass. Avoid using chemicals.
3 Keep hutch and run away from bonfires. Apart from the risk of fire, smoke may harm pets.
4 Keep the hutch away from the road to prevent escapes.
5 The soiled bedding can be used on the compost heap.
6 Trees can provide shade for the hutch, but falling branches could damage it.
7 If the hutch and run are visible from the house, any cats or dogs which appear to threaten the pets are seen.
8 A shed is useful for storing hay and food in suitable containers. Watch out for rodents.

has to be opened for recapturing each animal, there is an increased likelihood that the other occupants may slip out at the same time.

Siting the run
It is vital not to expose the animals to direct sunlight while in the run. Rabbits, especially, will die rapidly from heat stroke if there is no shade available. The temperature will rise rapidly under the plastic-covered part of the run, and because of this it may be worthwhile including a cardboard box at the opposite end to act as a temporary, cooler retreat. Both rabbits and guinea pigs will explore such boxes avidly, and often choose to rest inside, especially if they are lined with hay.

If possible, site the run on level ground, taking care that there are no poisonous plants in the grass which the animals might eat. Grass seed and turves are often treated with chemicals, so that a newly planted lawn may also prove dangerous. Also avoid placing the run on areas where weedkillers or chemicals have been used. On a safe patch, however, it is quite possible to keep an area of grass in trim by allowing rabbits or guinea pigs to graze it in sections at a time. Moving the run at intervals will also help to prevent killing the grass beneath the wooden part of the structure. The droppings can in turn act as a lawn fertilizer if left, although if you have dogs or young children in the family, it may be best to collect and dispose of the droppings by sweeping the grass using a stout-bristled brush.

Acclimatization
Once the weather is relatively fine and warm, the animals can stay in the run for much of the day, although it is probably better to transfer them back to their hutches at night. If greenfood has not already been fed regularly, however, rabbits especially should only be allowed access to the lawn for short periods. Otherwise they may consume excessive quantities of grass, which in turn is likely to cause scouring (diarrhoea.) Increasing the amount of greenfood gradually will allow the bacteria in the digestive tract to adjust over a period of time. It also serves to minimize the risk of bloat, which is caused by a build-up of gas in the intestinal tract. Bloat is almost impossible to cure, once the signs, notably a distended abdomen, are apparent. Since rabbits are prone to diarrhoea, try to avoid these risks as far as possible.

Left: *Various factors will influence the positioning of the hutch and run in the garden, as shown here. Local climatic factors are also very significant. Always pick a relatively shady part of the garden, since rabbits in particular are prone to heat stroke, which can rapidly prove fatal. Similarly, avoid placing the hutch in an exposed windy spot which would give the creatures little shelter during bad weather.*

Diet and feeding

Guinea pigs and rabbits are both herbivorous animals, but whereas the nutritional requirements of rabbits are well understood, less data is available for the precise needs of guinea pigs. It is known, however, that sufficient Vitamin C (ascorbic acid) must be present in the diet to meet their needs; otherwise the symptoms of scurvy will appear. All other mammals (with the exception of primates, including humans) are able to manufacture this vital vitamin in their bodies.

Vitamin C and guinea pigs

This distinction between the animals is particularly significant when housing rabbits and guinea pigs together, since rabbit food is not supplemented with Vitamin C, unlike the rations prepared for guinea pigs. A further complication arises because Vitamin C is a relatively unstable compound; it is therefore preferable to buy small quantities of food regularly. This will ensure that the guinea pig receives a relatively fresh diet containing the optimum level of Vitamin C, about 200mg per kg of food (approximately 90mg per lb). Check the expiry date recommended by the manufacturer if you buy the diet in packeted form: the maximum shelf life is likely to be no more than two or three months. Keeping the food in a cool, well-ventilated spot will help to prolong the vitamin content in prepared diets.

Apart from causing skin lesions, an early but unseen effect of Vitamin C deficiency is that it appears to render the body more susceptible to infections. Studies suggest that the average guinea pig weighing up to 1kg (2.2lb) requires 10mg of Vitamin C daily, while during pregnancy this figure can increase threefold. If the guinea pig appears unsteady on its feet and reluctant to walk, with haemorrhages evident in the mouth and elsewhere on the body, it may have a Vitamin C deficiency. Direct dietary supplement of the vitamin – usually as part of a multivitamin powder but, in severe cases, in tablet form – tends to be more satisfactory than giving it in drinking water, where it rapidly oxidizes and loses its potency. To be beneficial, a solution would need to contain at least 200mg of Vitamin C per litre (114mg per pint) of water, and should be changed once, possibly twice, daily. An added complication results if the water has been drawn through new copper pipes and so contains relatively high levels of this metal, since copper acts as a catalyst for the breakdown of Vitamin C.

Ensure that the condition never arises, therefore, by providing fresh greenstuff throughout the year. Broccoli is particularly valuable because it has a very high level of Vitamin C, averaging around 250mg per kg (114mg per lb). Also provide root vegetables, notably swedes and, to a lesser extent, carrots. These should be sufficient to keep your guinea pig healthy, especially when fed alongside a good-quality supplemented dry ration.

Fresh foods

You can offer a wide selection of fresh foods to rabbits and guinea pigs, depending partly on the time of year and where you live. Take care to ensure that all such foods are indeed fresh, and have not come from an area treated with toxic chemicals, or where other animals could have soiled them. Avoid collecting greenstuff from roadside verges for all these reasons, especially since the vegetation in many countries is likely to contain abnormally high levels of lead, from exhaust fume emissions. Wash all fresh foods thoroughly to remove any dirt before offering them to your animals.

If you have a garden, the best option is to set aside a small area in which to grow food for your pets, without fear of contamination. You can cultivate a range of vegetables as rabbit or guinea pig food and offer a variety of them on a regular basis. Rabbits especially will readily eat plants of the cabbage family, but excessive quantities may have a depressant effect on the thyroid glands. Therefore, alternate brassicas, as they are collectively known, with other items. Runner beans and peas, frequently described as legumes, are quite acceptable to both rabbits and guinea pigs and are often grown by keen gardeners. During the winter months, the choice is clearly more limited, but root vegetables such as turnip, swede and carrot are normally readily available and you can cut them into small pieces for feeding. Celery is also quite popular, as is sweet apple.

You can also offer your pets the leaves of some plants, provided that they have not wilted. This applies to all greenfood. Lettuce, which may seem an obvious choice, actually has very little nutritive value and may precipitate scouring (diarrhoea), particularly in rabbits, if fed in any quantity. Remember too that beetroot leaves contain oxalic acid and should not be fed, and that eating the root itself will lead to reddish urine, which under these circumstances is normal. Similarly, do not use potato plants for feeding. You can provide potatoes but be sure that they show no trace of green on their surface, as this is toxic. Potatoes should be boiled and offered either in small pieces or mashed, once they have cooled down. Not all individuals are keen on potato, however, and it can be messy when fed in a mashed form, even sticking to the fur.

Food from the wild
You can gather a variety of wild so-called weeds for feeding to either rabbits or guinea pigs. During periods of bad weather, when the animals are confined to their hutches, they will appreciate a handful of mixed grass clippings with the incorporated weeds. They prefer relatively short lawn grass to coarse, long meadow grass, however. The supply of wild plants will depend on the season, of course, with the greatest selection being available during spring and early summer. Do check before you feed any plants that they are not likely to be poisonous. If you are at all doubtful, the best approach is to ignore any plants unless you are absolutely sure they will not harm your stock. As a general guide, the following are all safe to use as food:

Bramble (*Rubus fruticosus*): Rabbits especially like the young leaves. You can also offer older leaves but take care that no thorns remain attached to the stalks if these too are fed. This is not a problem if one of the cultivated thornless varieties is available.

Below: *A combination of dried and fresh foods forms the ideal diet for rabbits and guinea pigs. Additional items, such as the round mineral block, may also be beneficial.*

Chickweed (*Stellaria media*): Various forms of chickweed exist and their distribution can be rather localized. It is a lush growing plant under good conditions, however, and produces tiny white flowers.

Clover (*Trifolium* species): Not an easy plant to gather in bulk, since it often occurs sporadically in an area of lawn and is normally fed with grass. It is also often present in hay.

Coltsfoot (*Tussilago farfara*) This plant and its flowers are readily taken by both rabbits and guinea pigs. Grows in all types of soil.

Dandelion (*Taraxacum officinale*): Easily cultivated from rootstock if desired. You can offer both the flowers and leaves, but preferably with other items, since this plant is said to have a laxative effect. As summer advances the leaves tend to die back and brown spots may appear on the surface. It is probably best to avoid leaves in this condition. Kept in a sheltered and moist environment, however, the plants continue to grow through much of the summer and well into the autumn. Other, similar plants which are normally available slightly later in the season are various forms of Sow-thistle (*Sonchus* sp.) and Nipplewort (*Lapsana communis*).

Groundsel (*Senecio vulgaris*): A common weed, which can act as a laxative, but is often contaminated with a white or reddish fungus on the undersides of the leaves. Do not use plants affected in this way for feeding to rabbits and guinea pigs.

Mallow (*Malva sylvestris*): More likely to be encountered in a rough area of grassland than in the average garden, but nevertheless useful for feeding purposes.

Plantain (*Plantago* species): Various forms are recognized, and the plants are sometimes described as 'Ratstails' because of their long seedheads which develop in late summer. Some types have broader leaves than others.

Shepherd's Purse (*Capsella bursa-pastoris*): Traditionally used by rabbit-keepers as a natural means of preventing scouring, this plant is quite distinctive when in flower. It has small white flowers, followed by

If you have access to a garden you will be able to obtain a variety of fresh foods. Always wash such foods before feeding, however, and avoid using chemical sprays, such as herbicides, if possible. Cultivating crops will provide fresh supplies throughout the year; these can be augmented with wild plants.

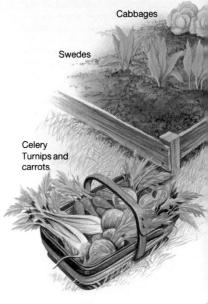

Cabbages

Swedes

Celery
Turnips and carrots

characteristic triangular seedpods on the central stem.

Yarrow (*Achillea millefolium*): Also known as Milfoil; this plant has delicate feathery leaves and a composite flowerhead. Yarrow is most obvious during late summer.

Edible garden flowers
Some of the flowers grown in gardens can also be valuable for feeding rabbits and guinea pigs. Among the annuals, Nasturtiums (*Tropaeolum majus*) and Sunflowers (*Helianthus annuus*) are valuable, especially for their leaves. Similarly, most individuals will readily eat Marigolds (*Tagetes* species), Asters (*Callistephus chinensis*) and Sweet Peas (*Lathyrus odoratus*). In the case of perennial plants, Golden Rod (*Solidago* species) and Michaelmas Daisies (*Aster* species)

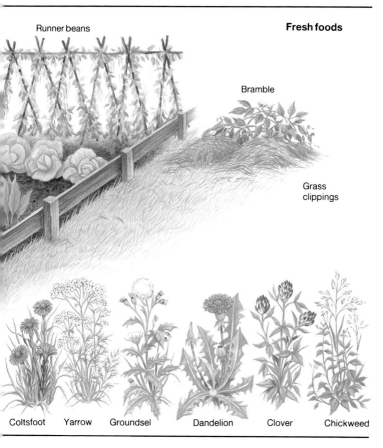

Runner beans

Fresh foods

Bramble

Grass clippings

Coltsfoot   Yarrow   Groundsel   Dandelion   Clover   Chickweed

are often greedily consumed, but check at the end of the flowering period that the leaves are not affected with mildew or a similar fungus, which shows as a white staining on the leaves.

Poisonous plants

A number of plants should never be used for feeding, as they are highly dangerous and may even be fatal for rabbits and guinea pigs. For example, never feed any flowers or leaves from bulbs, such as tulips. Other cultivated plants to avoid include Lily of the Valley (*Convallaria majalis*) and Laburnum (*Laburnum* species), as well as Lupins (*Lupinus* species).

Among common wild plants known to have toxic effects are Buttercups (*Ranunculus* species) and the aptly-named Deadly

Nightshade (*Atropa belladonna*). If in doubt about the identity of a particular plant, then do not use it. Hemlock (*Conium maculatum*) is a case in point: this particularly deadly plant is very similar in appearance to Hedge Parsley (*Anthriscus sylvestris*), which can be fed safely. Although you can distinguish Hemlock by its smooth, rather than grooved, stem, this is not always as apparent or easy as may be suggested.

Some small plants are especially dangerous because they may be fed inadvertently along with grass clippings or other greenfood. The Scarlet Pimpernel (*Anagallis arvensis*) is a good example: a relatively inconspicuous, low-growing plant with bright red flowers which only open in sunny weather, it will prove poisonous.

31

The actual effects of a harmful plant on the animal's body are various. Bracken (*Pteridum aquilinum*) destroys Vitamin B1 (thiamine) and this gives rise to characteristic nervous signs, while the bone marrow can also be affected. Symptoms do not become immediately apparent, as with Ragwort (*Senecio jacobaea*) poisoning, which primarily affects the liver. It may be possible to reverse the effects of poisoning in some cases, depending on the plant concerned, its effects and the quantity ingested, among other factors. The animal itself may reject a poisonous plant, especially if other food is available, but this cannot be guaranteed in all situations.

Hay
Many commercial breeding units do not offer their animals greenstuff, or indeed perishable foods of any kind, preferring instead to feed a commercially balanced ration of pellets. Even so, hay will usually feature in the feeding regimen. Hay provides more energy, and more protein, than the equivalent amount of grass from the same pasture. Although there may also be a significant difference between the various grades of hay in this regard, even the poorest hay tends to be better in nutritional terms than the equivalent amount of fresh grass.

The drying process which produces hay will also render safe for either guinea pigs or rabbits certain plants which, if fresh, would be dangerous. Buttercups (*Ranunculus* sp.) are a typical example. Nevertheless, keep a careful watch on the material you feed for undesirable plants and occasional harvesting debris. A strand of rusty barbed wire may get bound into a bale of hay from time to time, so remain alert and discard anything which potentially could be harmful. In the south-west of the United States, for example, close to the Pacific Ocean, the condition of Milkweed poisoning is seen in rabbit stocks. Also known as 'head-down disease' because it results in severe, if not fatal, paralysis, this illness is caused by ingesting the Woolly-pod Milkweed (*Asclepias eriocarpa*) from contaminated hay. In areas where such problems arise regularly, use an alternative bedding such as rice straw, so that the animals are not exposed to this risk.

Dry food and pellets
It is possible to keep rabbits and guinea pigs on a diet of essentially dry food, but in this case they will drink more water and may become overweight because of the regimen's high energy level. Suitable mixtures from your local pet store are likely to include crushed oats, flaked maize and wheat in equal quantities, plus smaller quantities of pellets and other ingredients such as crushed peas and locust bean pieces. While you can buy the individual ingredients separately and mix them together, it is probably best to

Below: *Research into the nutritional needs of rabbits has resulted in the formulation of pelleted diets, typically composed as shown here.*

Pellet composition
i.u. = International Units

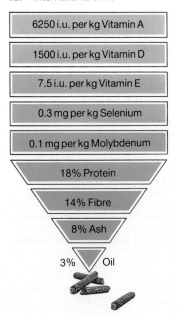

6250 i.u. per kg Vitamin A

1500 i.u. per kg Vitamin D

7.5 i.u. per kg Vitamin E

0.3 mg per kg Selenium

0.1 mg per kg Molybdenum

18% Protein

14% Fibre

8% Ash

3% Oil

obtain a prepared ration, which will be supplemented with Vitamin C for guinea pigs.

Pellets are specially made to contain all the necessary ingredients required for an animal's good health, and those for rabbits may even be medicated with drugs known as coccidostats. Do not feed medicated diets routinely, however, especially if the rabbit is kept alongside a guinea pig, as the drug may prove harmful to its companion. A pelleted ration provides a very concentrated food source and therefore only a small quantity will be required, otherwise the rabbit will become overweight quite rapidly.

Hard bread and mash

In order to keep the teeth of your animals in trim, provide bread which has been dried in an oven until it becomes very hard. Wholemeal bread is probably best for this purpose, with small pieces being given regularly.

Another useful food is a mash of some kind. Stored dry, mashes typically consist of bran and items such as middlings, a rough ground flour. Place the required quantity in a mixing dish with a small volume of warm water. Take care not to flood the mash, which ideally should be damp to the touch, but not mushy. You can include other available ingredients such as boiled or mashed potatoes or a powdered vitamin and mineral supplement. Once moist, however, the mash will not stay fresh for long, especially in a warm climate, and neither will perishable foods such as mashed potato, which will sour and turn black.

Feeding routine

Every owner will devise an individual routine, but rabbits and guinea pigs generally need feeding twice daily. In the morning, give them fresh foods, such as carrots, while in the afternoon, supply a bran mash and replenish the dry food as necessary.

Below: *Use a heavy pot, such as an earthenware bowl, as a dried food container. This proves quite stable and is easy to keep clean.*

On the following day, remove any remaining fresh food along with the mash, at the first feed.

A small flat tray is useful for offering fresh food. It makes the food easier to dispense and can also be washed between feeds. If you add detergent or disinfectant to the washing water, be sure to rinse the tray thoroughly, as with all feeding utensils. Although the animals are likely to drag some of the greenstuff on to their bedding, and may even retreat with it to their night quarters, the tray will help to prevent it becoming unnecessarily soiled on the hutch floor.

Rabbits in particular show a tendency to hurl feeding pots around their hutches, using their front teeth. So although you can try putting dry food and mashes on the stout plastic draining saucers produced for plant pots, it is probably better to opt for a heavier container. Light stainless steel bowls, although easy to clean thoroughly, are similarly less valuable, and the heavier glazed earthenware bowls sold in pet stores will prove most satisfactory. Commonly sold as drinking bowls for dogs, these are available in various sizes.

Water

Rabbits and guinea pigs both require a constant source of water, and this is best provided in a sealed vessel. An open bowl will soon become contaminated with hay, droppings and other debris from the lively scratching of the hutch's occupants. Special drinkers are now widely available, although they do differ slightly in design. Those with plastic rather than glass bottles are preferable since they are lighter and will not cause injury if accidentally dropped. The spout should be made of stainless steel; those made of plastic may be chewed over a period of time.

It is usual to hold the bottle in place with a loop of wire, which simply hooks over the mesh at the front of the hutch. Since the bottle sits at a slight angle, it exerts a considerable strain on the mesh,

especially when it is full. A determined rabbit can even dislodge its drinking bottle by pushing the spout back through the wire mesh. Although it may be more troublesome, it will be worthwhile attaching a second loop of wire to hold the bottle in place more securely. If a bottle does break, you may be able to obtain a replacement from the store, but generally you will have to buy a complete new drinker.

Change the water in the bottle every day as a rule, although you may need to vary this routine if you are using any kind of medication. It is inevitable that after a time, depending upon the light exposure, signs of algal growth will appear in the bottle as patches ranging from brown to green in colour. Wash the drinker every week, therefore, using a bottle brush to remove any traces of algae and to clean the entrance to the spout itself. Certain types of plastic drinkers are available in a tinted form; this will slow the development of algae on the sides of the container.

Apart from providing a reliable, clean supply of water, the major advantage of sealed drinkers is that they will not usually wet the bedding. If this does occur, the most likely reason is that the parts are not fitted together tightly enough; as a result no vacuum is formed in the bottle and the water simply runs through the spout. Alternatively, the animal may play repeatedly with the tip of the drinker, rather than actually consuming the fluid, so causing the leakage. This can be a difficult problem to overcome.

During the winter, if there is a risk of frost, do not fill the bottle right to the top. Leave a space for the water to expand into ice instead of cracking the sides of the bottle.

Right: *Feeding rabbits and guinea pigs is straightforward. Ensure that they have a supply of suitable dried food and fresh water constantly available. For guinea pigs, this needs to be supplemented with Vitamin C. Also offer fresh items regularly. Be sure to remove uneaten fresh food each day.*

Another cold weather problem is that although the main body of water may not be frozen, the small volume in the tip of the drinker may turn to ice, restricting or preventing the flow of fluid. Chilled water, or indeed greenfood, may cause an intestinal upset, and should be avoided if possible.

The actual fluid consumption of animals will vary, depending not only on temperature, but also on diet. Those feeding largely on dried foods will drink more water than individuals receiving a regular quantity of greenfood, which has a relatively high water content. A suckling female also drinks quite large volumes of water, in order to maintain her milk output. In large units, such as commercial breeding rabbitries, automatic drinking systems are likely to be in operation, but these are of little value to the average breeder. If necessary, you can give a breeding female an auxiliary water bottle, just in case the first supply becomes dislodged or blocked by particles of food debris, such as oats, deposited inside the end of the spout. Graduated drinking bottles make it easy to monitor the fluid intake of an individual or group, and this can be useful, especially if the animals concerned appear unwell.

Health care

Once established in its new home, a pet rabbit or guinea pig will usually prove a robust and relatively long-lived pet, whose care presents no particular difficulties. Rabbits and guinea pigs rank amongst the longest lived members of the group of small mammals typically kept as pets. Rabbits can live for as long as a decade, while guinea pigs may live into their eighth year under good conditions.

The short-haired breeds especially are very straightforward in their needs, and will not require any special grooming. One routine health care task that you may need to carry out is claw clipping.

Claw clipping

Claw clipping is largely a matter of experience; err on the side of caution at first, especially with dark-clawed individuals. It can be useful to have the rabbit on a bench, for example, and to ensure that someone else is on hand to restrain the animal's hindquarters while you concentrate on clipping the front claws. Restrain the paw with one hand while clipping, so that the animal cannot withdraw the nail, and work with each paw in succession. Animals with pale claws are more easy to deal with than those with black claws, since the red streak of the blood supply is more clearly visible in these animals.

Using bone clippers, cut the nail up to a short distance from the end of this streak. Only dead tissue will then be removed and there is no risk of bleeding. If bleeding does occur, it can usually be stopped quite easily by applying a styptic pencil to the end of the claw. Treat more serious wounds, such as those caused by fighting, with a solution of potash alum dissolved in cold water. These items should be on hand, along with the grooming

Clipping claws

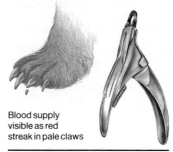

Blood supply visible as red streak in pale claws

Above: *Clipping a rabbit's claws. The first step is to restrain the animal and then locate the blood supply before actually cutting the claw.*

Below: *These clippers – with a precise guillotine action – are probably the easiest and safest type with which to clip claws.*

equipment – which is particularly vital for long-haired breeds – but there is no need to maintain a large medical chest for these animals.

Guinea pigs also need to have their claws clipped, but less frequently than rabbits.

The use of antibiotics

Both rabbits and guinea pigs are widely used for research purposes in laboratories around the world. As a result, a considerable amount of information is now available on the ailments to which these creatures are susceptible. Their reactions to drugs have also been studied extensively, with the discovery that the use of antibiotics, normally successful in combating bacterial infections, is often hazardous to these animals. Gut bacteria are essential in the digestion process of guinea pigs as well as rabbits, and the typical harmful effects of antibiotics on these bacteria are shown notably by penicillin.

Under normal circumstances, the guinea pig's intestine is lined by beneficial bacteria of the so-called Gram positive group. These, however, are killed by penicillin, so that harmful Gram negative bacteria establish themselves in the intestines and then spread through the body. The unfortunate animal dies about a week after receiving penicillin. Rabbits dosed with penicillin will suffer severe diarrhoea, but can survive; the related antibiotic, ampicillin, appears especially dangerous for them, however. Always seek veterinary advice before attempting to dose your ailing pet, especially in countries where antibiotics are readily available without a veterinary prescription. Never exceed the stated dose, as this too can have particularly catastrophic effects in rabbits and guinea pigs.

Quarantining stock

Rabbits and guinea pigs are prone to a number of diseases, which in certain instances can dramatically curb their lifespan. An animal living on its own is less at risk in this regard than the member of a constantly changing group of animals, as in a pet store. As a precaution, quarantine all new animals for at least a fortnight, and preferably three weeks, before introducing them into an established group.

If you are buying a new animal for breeding purposes, it is vital to remember that some individuals can be symptomless carriers of particular infections, such as pasturellosis in the case of rabbits. Disease may be well established in a colony, but not become apparent until the animals are stressed in some way, perhaps by being moved to a new environment.

The remainder of this section forms a brief survey of common infections and parasitic diseases that may affect rabbits and guinea pigs in captivity.

Bacterial diseases

Many of the most common diseases are caused by bacteria of various kinds. Here, we consider a range of bacterial infections and how they can be prevented and treated.

Pasturellosis is certainly one of the most widespread diseases of rabbits, and can give rise to a variety of symptoms in areas ranging from the respiratory system to the genital tract. Even wounds caused by fighting will be readily infected by *Pasturella* bacteria, and the outcome can well be fatal within a couple of days. Often, however, the most common manifestation of *Pasturella* in a group of rabbits is the disease described as 'snuffles'.

The most obvious sign of this ailment will be a discharge from the nose as well as the eyes. In an attempt to clear the disorder, a rabbit will paw constantly at its face, causing its feet to become stained with the discharge, and may sneeze repeatedly. Such signs are most likely to be apparent if the rabbit is stressed; they can disappear almost spontaneously in some cases, although the infection is still likely to be present within the respiratory system. In a few instances, however, the infection may spread to give rise to middle ear disease,

Above: *Moist staining of the paws can indicate snuffles as the rabbit attempts to wipe the discharges.*

Above: *Discharges from nose and eyes associated with snuffles are usually caused by* Pasturella.

which interferes with the rabbit's sense of balance. One of the typical signs will be torticollis, when the unfortunate animal's neck is held at an abnormal angle. It is difficult to treat pasturellosis successfully in any event, but once the middle ear infection of otitis media develops, then the animal should be painlessly destroyed.

Elsewhere in the body, *Pasturella* may localize in the reproductive tract of both sexes. It can cause infertility in the doe if both horns of the uterus are affected. The buck may develop inflamed testicles, and a discharge from the penis will be apparent in some cases. A vaginal discharge is relatively common in does, but bucks may sometimes be symptomless carriers and these represent a particular danger if they are used for mating on a regular basis. The bacteria can remain in the prostate gland, for example, and be expelled into the doe's tract during mating, when prostate secretions perform a vital role in nourishing the spermatozoa after ejaculation has occurred. This is a particularly difficult condition to treat with antibiotics, so do not use any bucks for breeding if you suspect they may be infected with *Pasturella*, otherwise the bacteria can spread through a stud very quickly.

Pseudotuberculosis, also known as yersiniosis because it is caused by the bacterium *Yersinia pseudotuberculosis*, is not, in fact, related to tuberculosis, although the post-mortem signs associated with both diseases are similar. Both rabbits and guinea pigs will succumb to the illness, which can be spread by mice and other rodents visiting their cages, although contaminated foodstuffs are more commonly blamed for outbreaks. The disease is not rapidly fatal in most cases; affected animals simply appear vaguely ill and often off their food at first. Other signs, including weight loss, diarrhoea and laboured breathing, will subsequently become apparent. The liver, spleen, lungs and other organs are affected, as are the lymph nodes throughout the body, which swell in size.

There is no realistic treatment available, and painlessly destroying the animal is the best option, especially since yersiniosis is a zoonotic infection, i.e. one which can spread to humans. Seek

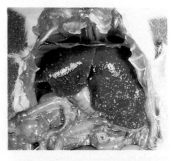

Above: *White spots evident on the liver from pseudotuberculosis. Treatment is not practical.*

veterinary advice if you suspect the disease, and wash out the hutch thoroughly afterwards, using an approved disinfectant as directed. Affected animals may survive for a month, during which time they can be a threat to the health of their owners. From all standpoints, therefore, you should take immediate action.

Enzootic cervical lymphadenitis is a disease of guinea pigs which affects the lymph nodes, and young animals are most susceptible. It is caused by the bacterium known as the β-haemolytic *Streptococcus*, belonging to the Lancefield Type C group. Streptococci of other types can also be responsible, gaining access to the body through a cut, or simply through an abrasion in or close to the mouth. Sharp, unsuitable bedding, such as oat or wheat straw, may cause the initial wound. From here, the bacteria reach the lymphatic system and localize in the lymph nodes around the head. The first external sign is likely to be a distinct swelling on the lower part of the jaw, or close to the top of the neck. In some cases, more than one gland can be affected. The bacteria may also spread rapidly around the rest of the body, affecting a variety of organs, such as the heart, lungs and liver. The outcome then is fatal, but if you suspect the disease early enough, a veterinarian may be able to contain it with antibiotic injections.

There is a particular danger if the swellings rupture, since the discharge will be highly infectious. Indeed, you should keep any animals showing symptoms in separate accommodation. It is safest to handle them when necessary using disposable gloves. Also take particular care to ensure that their food pots and water containers are kept apart from those of healthy stock and washed separately. Such precautions apply, of course, in all cases when dealing with a sick guinea pig or rabbit.

Salmonellosis is not a common disease, but again can be

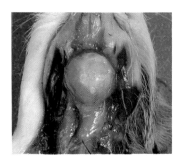

Above: *A case of enzootic cervical lymphadenitis, with the swollen lymph nodes visible in the neck.*

introduced by infected rodents, contaminated bedding materials or foodstuffs. It can be difficult to diagnose even an acute case, as death can occur with few if any signs appearing within two days of the bacteria being ingested. Good management is therefore vital in preventing this infection of the digestive system, which is another that can be transmitted to humans.

Pneumonia can affect both rabbits and guinea pigs, the illness resulting from either bacterial or viral causes. Although pneumonia may lead to the rapid death of the animal, it can also be a chronic condition. The latter is the case with streptococcal pneumonia, for which *Diplococcus pneumoniae* is often the bacterium responsible. Affected guinea pigs can show various signs, including reddish urine caused by the presence of blood. As a similar coloration of the urine can result from dietary causes, however, notably the feeding of beetroot, this is not a diagnostic sign on its own.

In rabbits, *Pasturella* bacteria are a common cause of pneumonia. Poor environmental conditions, particularly dirty, damp hutches, will predispose an animal to pneumonia. Antibiotic treatment may be worthwhile if the condition is recognized early. Loss of appetite, linked with a raised temperature of around 40°C (104°F), tends to be indicative of pneumonia in rabbits, especially when coupled with rapid breathing as one of the signs.

Schmorl's disease is another ailment commonly seen in rabbits kept under dirty conditions. It may also be linked to a superficial injury, which permits the *Fusobacterium* to gain access to the body. Although similar to enzootic cervical lymphadenitis seen in guinea pigs, there is often a closer link with a skin injury, and the obvious signs of infection – swellings around the face, abscesses and ulceration – can therefore be more widespread over the surface of the body. Similar treatment applies.

Vent disease, a venereal disease of rabbits, is reasonably obvious, since it leads to hair loss around the vent region. The infection is caused by *Treponema cunicula* and at first gives rise to clear blister-like swellings, which ultimately form scabs. These can also spread directly to the face, notably the eyelids and lips, and animals which are obviously infected should be kept on their own. Do not use them for breeding purposes, since this is how the disease is spread. Medical treatment using antibiotics can prove valuable in overcoming the infection and it usually clears up after about two weeks. A successfully treated rabbit no longer presents a danger to others in the stud and can be safely used for breeding.

Hutch burn can cause similar symptoms to vent disease, yet the former is primarily caused by bad management, when rabbits are kept in wet, insanitary surroundings. Their acid urine damages the skin around the genital area, and bacteria cause the formation of scabs. The hocks, those parts of the legs in contact with the ground, are sometimes similarly affected. This problem can also occur with rabbits being kept in wire pens, if the mesh floor is unsuitable. Most susceptible are the Rex breeds, since they have a relatively thin covering of fur on the undersides of their hocks; this breed must have adequate bedding at all times. Clearly, however, it is vital to prevent the condition from

occurring by ensuring that environmental conditions are satisfactory in all cases.

Dental and digestive disorders
If a rabbit appears unable to eat, first look at its mouth to see if the incisor teeth are overgrown, giving rise to the condition known as dental malocclusion or 'buck teeth'. Your veterinarian will cut the teeth back for you, although it is possible to carry out this task yourself. First obtain a pair of bone clippers – scissors are not really suitable – and ask someone to hold the rabbit for you on a table or similar level surface. Then prise open the mouth and, holding the jaws, clip the teeth. Do not be tempted to cut the teeth too short; simply remove the twisted area of growth. Offering chewing blocks, or even dried crusts of bread, may help to slow down growth of the incisors, but within a few weeks you will almost certainly need to clip the teeth again.

Dribbling of saliva from the mouth, known as 'slobbers', may also be caused by a dental problem. The most noticeable sign is likely to be an area of wet fur at the corner of the mouth, with possible swelling around the side of the face if a tooth abscess is the cause of the complaint. A closer veterinary examination will be essential for this problem, and the rabbit may have to be anaesthetized. Using modern drugs, this is a relatively safe procedure, as it is for guinea pigs.

Above: *A severe case of overgrown teeth. Regular trimming will ensure that the rabbit can eat normally.*

Diarrhoea and enteritis While the effects of drugs are well studied in rabbits, much work is still required to discover why these animals appear so susceptible to diarrhoea. The problem is usually complex, involving more than one infectious agent. Yet it does appear that stress of any kind is significant, and that young animals are most at risk.

The signs of mucoid enteritis will typically be seen in rabbits up to about five months of age, with a peak likely around the two to three month period. Affected animals lose their appetites and grow listless. Diarrhoea, often clear and jelly-like, rapidly becomes apparent, together with an accompanying high level of water consumption. An accumulation of gas in the abdomen may give rise to the characteristic swelling described as bloat, and death will occur within about a week of the symptoms first appearing. Where large numbers of rabbits are at risk, the use of medicated foods may be advisable through this crucial period. Once the disease does occur, however, the likelihood of recovery is relatively slight; and even if they do survive, affected individuals may remain stunted.

Part of the difficulty with treatment is that there appears to be no single cause of mucoid enteritis. Bacteria, including members of the costridial group, are known to be involved in most cases. In addition, *Bacillus piliformis*, which is responsible for Tyzzer's Disease, can be identified in cases of mucoid enteritis. Tyzzer's Disease is recognized as a separate ailment affecting even younger rabbits, normally about six weeks old. It invariably proves fatal at this stage, with symptoms similar to mucoid enteritis.

If rabbits do die from enteritis of any kind, thoroughly clean and disinfect their quarters to minimize the risk of spreading the disease. Also dispose of their bedding, preferably by burning it. When faced with a sudden, explosive outbreak of this problem, consult a veterinarian without delay. It will be possible to carry out post-mortems, and from the results of these plus other tests, notably those to find the bacteria concerned, it may be feasible to treat surviving stock.

Protozoan parasites causing diarrhoea While it is unclear what part viruses play in causing diarrhoea in rabbits, it is known that unicellular parasites called coccidia are frequently involved. These protozoa can only be seen under the microscope, and can have a variety of effects. Some rabbits become carriers of the disease known as coccidosis, and represent a considerable danger to other animals likely to be susceptible. The intestinal form of coccidosis can be caused by various *Eimeria* protozoa. Diarrhoea, poor growth rate and a loss of appetite are all associated symptoms.

The life cycle of these disease-causing protozoa is relatively complex. Since the infective stage is voided in the droppings, spread is less common among stock held in wire-floored cages because the droppings fall through the mesh out of reach of the rabbits and their food. Good hygiene therefore helps to prevent the spread of this disease, while medicated rations incorporating a drug called a coccidostat are used commercially in some countries. Certain disinfectants will destroy the oocysts passed in the faeces. It is also possible to screen rabbit droppings to see if they are carrying coccidosis, but such sophisticated techniques are more feasible for the breeder than for the pet-owner.

In some cases, intestinal coccidosis can also cause a nasal form of the disease. This happens because the rabbit consumes its own faeces. The oocysts in the droppings are introduced to the mucous lining of the nose, where they develop and cause a discharge. Even if a rabbit recovers, the intestinal lining may be permanently damaged and so impair the absorption of foodstuffs.

A form of coccidosis affecting the liver can give rise to external signs similar to those caused by the *Eimeria* species. The severity of this illness, called hepatic coccidosis, can be directly related to the number of oocysts which were consumed in the first instance. Sulphur-based drugs given in either food or water can prevent clinical signs of the disease appearing, and may also be used for treatment. Hepatic coccidosis can prove fatal, however, and can become a serious problem if an infected individual is introduced to a susceptible group.

Guinea pigs can also be affected by coccidosis, but in these animals the disease tends to be less severe, and is rarely fatal. The protozoan responsible, *Eimeria caviae*, can again be detected in the guinea pig's droppings. Signs are likely to be non-specific, including diarrhoea and loss of appetite.

Occasionally, other protozoa can also be found. *Encephalitozoon cuniculi* is the most significant of these, causing the disease nosematosis. It can affect both rabbits and guinea pigs, localizing in the kidneys and brain, producing neurological disturbances but rarely obvious symptoms. The urine can be infectious, however, and the disease can also spread across the placenta to unborn young.

Other internal parasites

Intestinal worms are not usually a significant problem in either guinea pigs or rabbits, but rabbits do act as the intermediate host in the life cycle of both dog and cat tapeworms. In the wild, the dog voids segments of the tapeworm which in turn contaminate pasture. The eggs may then be ingested with greenfood by a browsing rabbit. In the body of the rabbit, the tapeworm egg develops into a larva within a fluid-filled cyst, which can create a large swelling visible on the animal's body. In the wild, when a dog catches and eats the rabbit, the tapeworm can undergo the final stage of its development into a mature parasite, thus completing the cycle.

This final stage is unlikely to take place in a domestic environment, but a pet rabbit grazing in its run on a lawn shared with a dog or cat can certainly develop a larval cyst. The key to controlling the problem is to remove the adult tapeworms from the gut of the dog or cat by regular deworming. The most effective treatments of this type are available from a veterinarian, who will also provide dosage instructions. Discourage any dog or cat from defecating on the lawn where the rabbit has its run, so as to minimize the risk of infection. Always wash all greenfood and vegetables thoroughly, to ensure that they are not contaminated with dog or cat excrement. If a cyst does occur, a veterinarian may be able to remove it.

External parasites

External parasites found on the body do not have as complex a life cycle as tapeworms, but tend to be spread by direct contact.

Mites Ear mites (notably *Psoroptes cuniculi*) give rise to canker in rabbits, which is an intensely irritating condition. An affected rabbit will paw repeatedly at its ears, maybe causing itself further damage. The signs of canker are unmistakable: instead of appearing clean and free from debris, the insides of the ears are full of brownish crusts. It is important to deal with this condition as soon as possible, since it can spread into the inner ear and give rise to neurological symptoms, which are

Below: *A guinea pig with clear signs of mite infestation of the skin. Medicated shampoos are effective.*

likely to be irreversible. For this reason, never attempt to remove the deposits simply by scraping them away, as pieces will fall deeper into the ear canal. In any event this will probably cause bleeding, apart from being painful.

Various remedies will successfully kill off the mites responsible for canker, allowing the condition to heal gradually so that a full recovery can be anticipated. See your veterinarian in order to obtain treatment, although in an emergency you can use one of the proprietary products sold in pet stores for the treatment of cats' ears. The traditional remedy is to apply flowers of sulphur to the ear, and this yellow powder can still be found in some pharmacies. Apart from treating the affected rabbit, wash its quarters out thoroughly to ensure that any surviving mites present in skin debris are killed, otherwise reinfection may occur. Although all breeds are susceptible, the Lop-eared varieties, with their large pendulous ears, are probably more at risk from this ailment than relatively short-eared breeds, such as the Netherland Dwarf.

Skin complaints are quite often encountered in guinea pigs, and one common cause is mite infestation. The first sign of infection is likely to be minute white spots, where the mites have burrowed into the skin. The coat becomes thin and full of whitish scurf, resembling dandruff. It can be difficult to distinguish between this and other skin ailments, however, including hair loss and skin damage resulting from ringworm, so seek veterinary advice without delay. A veterinarian may take a skin scraping to confirm the diagnosis, and can then prescribe effective treatment to kill the mites.

As a guinea pig living on its own may develop the infection, it seems likely that these mites can be introduced on bedding material. Alternatively, the infection could be transferred from a sow to offspring, remaining latent until triggered by certain factors, such as stress. Treatment is likely to require partial washing of the guinea pig with a special shampoo, a task which you will probably have to repeat after a fortnight. Again, you will need to scrub out the hutch to kill off any surviving mites. The shampoo prescribed for the guinea pig may also be suitable for washing out the hutch, although the dilution factor can vary. Discuss this with your veterinarian.

The most significant mite infestation affecting either rabbits or guinea pigs is caused by *Cheyletiella parasitivorax*, a relatively large mite. Hair loss, dandruff and crustiness of the skin are typical signs of the mange it causes. Although it occurs mainly on wild rabbits, it may occasionally spread to domestic pets, and is capable of living away from a host, which aids its spread. This disease is highly infectious, and can be spread to or from other domestic pets, including cats and dogs. Humans may also develop symptoms, so if you suspect that your pet could be suffering from this parasite, handle it carefully using gloves. The condition is not difficult to treat successfully, but repeated medication may be necessary.

Lice and fleas Lice, unlike mites, spend the whole of their life cycle on their host, and their egg-cases or 'nits' are most likely to be seen in the fur along the animal's back. These are not common, especially if the animals are kept in clean surroundings, but when apparent you can eliminate them by using a similar preparation to that recommended for dealing with skin mites. Fleas are extremely rare in domestic stock, although they may occur on wild rabbits.

Maggots Among the parasites most dangerous to rabbits and guinea pigs are the larvae of various common flies. The adult fly will lay eggs in organic matter, being especially attracted to the rear end of rabbits suffering from scour, since the fur in this region will be contaminated with faecal matter. The larvae hatch rapidly and then actually bore into the animal's tissue

– so-called 'fly strike'. This can lead to the speedy development of bacterial disease, while the larvae themselves produce a toxin which can have deadly effects, especially if the animal is already weakened.

Clearly, this problem is more likely to arise during warm weather, and stock at risk should be inspected daily as a matter of course. In order to minimize the threat, you may need to clip off heavily soiled fur. This will certainly be necessary if maggots do become established. Clean the affected area as thoroughly as possible, and remove the maggots with forceps. Then dust the site with a wound powder, as recommended by your veterinarian, and this will also help to dry up secretions from the damaged tissue.

A possible preventative measure involves fitting a very fine mesh at the front of the cage, in order to stop flies gaining access to a susceptible animal. You can attach the mesh to the wooden framework of the door with drawing pins. If you then tape all the edges, there will be no access for flies around this false front.

Ringworm In spite of its name, this is not a parasitic disease, but results from infection by a fungus, usually *Trichophyton*. Although not very common in either rabbits or guinea pigs, cases can arise in pet stores, for example, where young kittens previously infected have been housed in the same accommodation. The spores of the fungus are very durable. They can survive for months in the environment before infecting rabbits or guinea pigs later kept in the same pens as the infected animals, especially if these have not been thoroughly cleaned.

Ringworm can affect humans, producing characteristic reddish circular patches on the skin, typically on the forearms. Similar signs, linked with hair loss, can be seen when it affects rabbits and guinea pigs. Treatment is possible but protracted, requiring at least a fortnight of daily dosing. In order to kill off any surviving spores, either

scrub the surface of the hutch using an approved disinfectant, or play a blow-torch over the surfaces, taking great care not to set fire to the hutch.

Viral diseases
Relatively little is known about viral diseases in guinea pigs. In rabbits, mxyomatosis is a key viral disease.

Myxomatosis This is without doubt the best known and most notorious viral disease to affect rabbits. It was actually used as a means of controlling rabbit populations after the virus itself had been initially identified in South American rabbits. These animals had developed a virtual immunity to the disease and rarely displayed signs of infection, although they acted as carriers for the virus. When introduced to susceptible rabbits, it invariably proved fatal. The virus can be spread by direct contact and by insects, notably mosquitos and the rabbit flea (*Spillopsyllus cuniculi*).

On being liberated in Europe in 1952, myxomatosis had an initially devastating effect on the wild rabbit population, but has since become a relatively benign infection. Surviving stocks now tend to be symptomless carriers of the virus, like their South American counterparts. Domestic stocks have not, however, been exposed to the virus and remain highly susceptible. Mosquitos may transmit the disease from wild rabbits, or it may spread directly in areas with a high population of wild

Above: *This rabbit shows the typical signs of myxomatosis, for which there is no treatment. It is possible to protect stock by vaccination.*

rabbits, which can be attracted to the hutches or runs.

The earliest sign of myxomatosis is likely to be conjunctivitis ('pink-eye'), followed by a milky discharge from the eye. Affected rabbits then lose their appetites, and their body temperature rises rapidly, from about 39.5°C (103°F) to 42°C (108°F). Death follows soon afterwards. In less acute cases, the rabbit becomes increasingly inert; swellings develop around the face, notably affecting the lips, eyes and ears, which tend to droop as a result. The genital area may also be affected, and there is a discharge from the nostrils in most cases. The incubation period of the disease is approximately five days, and death occurs usually within a fortnight of the rabbit becoming ill. Once signs are apparent, you should contact your veterinarian, who will dispose of the animal humanely without delay.

There is no effective treatment for myxomatosis, which can have devastating effects on a rabbit stud. As a result, breeders may have their susceptible stock inoculated with a live vaccine, which affords good protection. Hutches raised 60cm (24in) off the ground will ensure that wild rabbits cannot reach their domestic counterparts, and this precaution can help prevent the spread of the disease. After an outbreak has occurred, thorough disinfection is again required, for the virus can spread easily through discharges from ruptured swellings.

Other disorders
The following disorders are all non-infectious, but can cause problems.

Wool eating Even the best-run studs may have a rabbit which proves to be a wool eater. It is normal for a doe to pull some hair to create a nest, but this activity can sometimes become a pathological complaint. Quantities of hair will then be swallowed and may create an internal blockage, notably in the stomach. A laxative will hopefully clear the obstruction, but wool eating tends to become a habit, for which there is no cure.

Rectal impaction This problem affecting the digestive tract is typically seen in older guinea pigs, especially boars. First you may notice that the animal is not defecating normally. Closer exmination reveals a large swelling of the walls of the rectum, with a solid mass of faeces within. It is a most unpleasant condition, but if this blockage is gently squeezed out, the guinea pig appears unconcerned and can live quite happily. You will have to repeat the procedure regularly, however, because the muscular walls of the rectum lose their efficiency, thereby creating the blockage.

Vitamin and mineral imbalances
Vitamin E, together with the trace element selenium, is necessary for the correct functioning of skeletal muscular tissue. Guinea pigs are susceptible to a dietary shortage of this vitamin, and when such a situation occurs, will become inert, only moving stiffly when encouraged to do so. It is a relatively rare condition in rabbits, but can cause high mortality in newly born offspring, while the reproductive rate of the does also declines. Providing a vitamin and mineral supplement, either in powder form or in a block, will help prevent such deficiencies, especially if the animals are receiving a balanced diet. Vitamin C deficiency in guinea pigs is discussed on page 28.

An excess or imbalance between vitamins and minerals can also have harmful effects, producing in guinea pigs the condition known as metastatic calcification. Boars appear most at risk, with the disease appearing in stock over a year old. The problem arises when calcium becomes deposited at various abnormal sites in the body, such as the kidneys, heart and liver. Sudden death can occur as a result, with few preceding symptoms, although the condition can be easily detected at post-mortem. It can also be confirmed using X-rays on living animals if necessary. A change in diet will prevent a recurrence; discuss this with your veterinarian.

Choosing between a rabbit and a guinea pig as a pet can be difficult. For children, guinea pigs may be a better option, being more compact and easier to handle as a result. Children also find the sounds of guinea pigs attractive; their characteristic high-pitched 'oinking' call at the anticipation of being fed tends to create a friendly appeal. Although less likely to scratch, guinea pigs may also prove more nervous, however, depending on whether they have been handled from an early age.

Rabbits and guinea pigs are equally easy to cater for, and cost about the same, although guinea pigs can be housed in smaller quarters than rabbits, especially the giant breeds. On the other hand, rabbits certainly present a greater variety of choice in terms of coat coloration and texture, as well as size. The Angora breed is especially notable for its wool, which is used to make clothes!

Once you have made your choice, be sure to use a stout card-

board box to transport your pet home. Ideally this should close with flaps to provide security, especially for a guinea pig, which will be very nervous unless it can hide away beneath a covering of hay. Bear in mind that if a rabbit urinates while in its travelling box – as is likely since it will probably be unused to travelling in this way – the cardboard may become saturated and no longer support the weight of the animal. In any event, it is worth tying the box securely with string. Once home, never leave an open box on a table or bench; if the rabbit climbs out or, more likely, tips the box over by leaning on a side, it is likely to end up on the floor. Falls of this type can prove especially harmful to rabbits, and can result in spinal injury or paralysis, for which there is no cure. If you need to restrain your pet, always place it in a basket with the lid firmly shut. Cat baskets are useful for this purpose, although special carrying boxes may be used for exhibition stock and also for transporting pet animals.

Rabbits

There are now over 100 breeds of domestic rabbit, which can weigh on average about 1-4kg (2.2-8.8lb). Many rabbits sold in pet stores belong to no particular breed, or are simply poorly marked individuals that would not be suitable for exhibition purposes, but nevertheless make endearing pets. Before we look at the breeds of show rabbits, we will consider how to breed rabbits in general.

Breeding

Breeding rabbits is a relatively straightforward procedure, but should not be carried out haphazardly. Before breeding rabbits, consider carefully how you will dispose of the young. There is no guarantee, for example, that the local pet store will willingly take a litter of perhaps ten or more offspring.

The age of maturity in rabbits depends to some extent on the breed concerned. Smaller breeds, such as the Dutch, become mature as early as eighteen weeks and most medium-sized breeds can be bred successfully by the time they are twenty-two weeks old. The giant breeds are the slowest to mature, and may not be sexually competent until they are nine months old.

The breeding habits of the rabbit differ from those of most mammals in that the doe has no regular oestrus cycle. Instead, she is described as being an induced ovulator, meaning that she can be stimulated to produce ova simply by being placed with a buck. Indeed, a problem that commonly occurs when keeping does together is that this in itself can trigger ovulation, and serves to encourage the development of so-called false pregnancies, when the doe shows the typical signs of pregnancy although she has not in fact mated with a buck.

Below: *Female rabbits construct a nest for their offspring, pulling their own wool to create a soft lining. Smaller breeds will mature earlier than the larger breeds.*

Rabbit nesting box

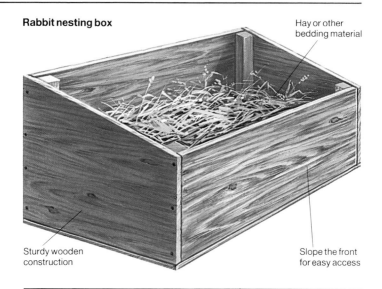

Hay or other bedding material

Sturdy wooden construction

Slope the front for easy access

Above: *Some breeders like to provide a nesting box where the doe can give birth and raise her litter through the early stages. Adjust the size of the box to the breed.*

Mating

When mating is desired, check the genital area of the doe. If she is ready to breed, the skin will be quite red, rather than pale pink. It is usual to transfer her to the buck's cage, and leave them together.

Assuming both animals are in good condition, mating normally occurs quite soon afterwards. A buck will be capable of mating several times during the course of a week, but do not encourage this more than necessary, especially with a young buck, if a high level of fertility is to be maintained.

After mating, house the doe on her own and provide her with an appropriate nesting box. Several days before the birth, the doe will prepare a nest for her litter, lining it with hair pulled from her body. This process is described as kindling in the case of rabbits.

If you require another litter from a particular doe, remating can take place from six to eight weeks after the preceding litter was born. After an unsuccessful mating, however, a false pregnancy can arise. The doe will then attempt to build a nest as early as the seventeenth day after mating. Once it is clear that the doe is not pregnant, she can be remated. Under normal circumstances, it is possible to detect pregnancy by carefully feeling the abdomen twelve days after mating, when the foetuses will be apparent. The most noticeable increase in size does not occur until the last week, however. It is better not to interfere and handle the doe excessively, but allow nature to take its course. In most cases, things run quite smoothly.

Rearing

The gestation period lasts about thirty-one days and the young are then born naked. An average litter consists of between six and nine offspring. After a successful birth, avoid disturbing the nest if all appears to be going well, especially in the case of a maiden doe with a first litter. Excessive interference at this stage can lead to the doe neglecting her litter or, worse still, cannibalizing the offspring. When inspecting the nest, touch the doe first so as to transfer her scent to your hands; in this way she will be less disturbed by the process.

Young rabbits grow rapidly, and their fur will appear by the fourth day. Their eyes should be open by nine days, and they will start to leave their nest about a week later. By the age of one month, the young rabbits will be almost independent. If you are ringing the young for exhibition purposes, do this when they are being weaned, before the ankle joint grows too big to slide the ring over.

Problems can arise during the rearing period, and you may hear the young rabbits calling if they are distressed or short of food. If this happens, first check the doe to see if she is suffering from an infection of the nipples, called mastitis. In this state, the glands are at first red and tender, but rapidly turn blue, when the condition is described as 'blue breast'. Treatment can be very difficult once infection is advanced and, to complicate matters, it is difficult to hand rear orphan rabbits successfully. Therefore, consult a veterinarian without delay if you suspect that your doe could be suffering from mastitis.

In terms of nutritional balance, the best substitute for doe's milk is goat's milk, which may be available from a healthfood store. Give this to the youngsters by means of a feeding dropper, which can be acquired from a pharmacist. It is not possible, however, to compensate effectively for the natural immunity which a doe transfers to her offspring in the form of antibodies. This leaves orphaned rabbits at increased risk from infection until their own immune systems are fully operational at weaning.

Right: *The butterfly markings of this day-old Dwarf Lop are clearly apparent even at this early stage. Avoid disturbing the nest unnecessarily, since the doe is very sensitive during this period. Excessive interference is likely to cause her to neglect and possibly even cannibalize her offspring. Always touch her first, therefore, so that your hands carry her scent before picking up the young rabbits.*

Parents

Homozygous
Satin Coat

Genetics in action (1). This diagram shows the likely percentages of offspring that can be anticipated when pairing a Normal Coated rabbit with a Satin Coated. In genetical terms, the Satin is recessive to the Normal Coated so that all the offspring in the first generation appear Normal Coated, yet they also carry the Satin gene in their make-up. It is possible to distinguish them by a test mating.

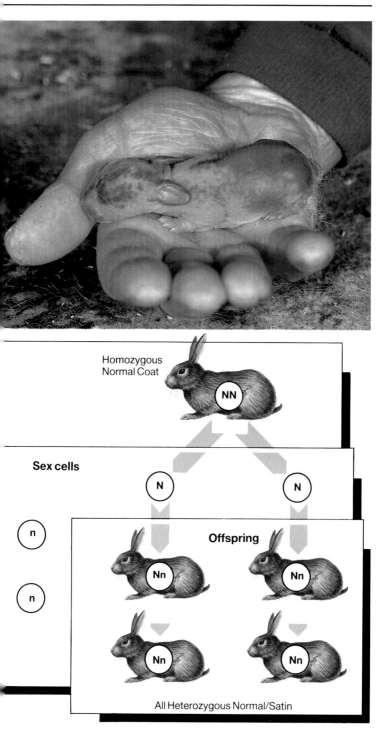

Homozygous
Normal Coat

Sex cells

Offspring

All Heterozygous Normal/Satin

Show rabbits

Show rabbits can be broadly divided into two basic categories, known as fur and fancy. The so-called fur breeds tend to be of more recent origin. They are viewed as multipurpose and can be kept for food, for example, as well as for the quality of their fur. The fancy breeds are the more traditional show rabbits, among which well-marked specimens are highly valued. Within each particular breed, there may be different colours: such differences are described as varieties. The following is a selection of the most popular breeds and varieties of rabbits seen internationally.

Alaska

Bred originally in Germany, this is a striking but scarce black breed, with a predominantly shiny, silky coat. It should have a rather dumpy, thickset appearance, and weigh around 3.6kg (8lb). The Alaska was derived essentially from Himalayan and Argente stock, while Dutch stock may also have figured in its development. The eyes and claws of the Alaska must also be dark, reflecting the colour of its fur.

Parents

Heterozygous
Normal/Satin

Nn

Genetics in action (2). Here the results of pairing two carriers of the Satin gene can be seen, with their offspring receiving one gene from each parent. In this case, approximately one quarter of the offspring will be Satin, i.e. with two recessive genes, whereas the remaining offspring will resemble Normals. In reality, the majority will be heterozygous, carrying the Satin genes like their parents.

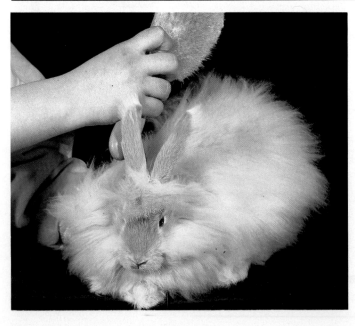

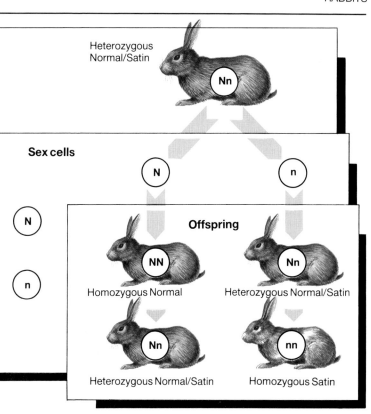

Heterozygous Normal/Satin
Nn

Sex cells

N

n

N

n

Offspring

NN
Homozygous Normal

Nn
Heterozygous Normal/Satin

Nn
Heterozygous Normal/Satin

nn
Homozygous Satin

American Checkered Giant
This is a show breed for the specialist, since the standard for these particular rabbits is very demanding. The markings are considered extremely significant. It is related to the butterfly breeds from Europe, and reflects this ancestry in the winged markings that should be apparent on the face. These extend from lip to lip over the nose, where the outline of a butterfly's body should be discernible. Blue and black varieties of the American Checkered Giant are officially recognized. It is a large breed, as its name suggests, weighing around 5.5kg (12lb).

Left: *Grooming an Angora rabbit, an essential part of preparing this handsome breed for a show. Such show breeds may not be entirely suitable as pets because of the amount of coat care they need.*

The American
This popular breed was developed in the United States during the early years of the 20th century. The initial stock was blue, but a white variety emerged and was ultimately accepted for show purposes. There is also a difference in eye coloration: the white is an albino and so has pink eyes, whereas those of the blue match the coloration of the coat. Other colours are not acceptable for exhibition purposes.

The Heavy variety of this breed weighs up to 4.5kg (10lb) and the Giant up to 6.8kg (15lb).

Angevin
This truly giant breed was said to have an overall length of 1.5m (5ft) and to weigh over 10kg (22lb). Known as long ago as the 16th century, it is now extinct but probably played a role in the ancestry of today's large breeds.

Angora

The origins of this unique and old breed have been lost. It may have originated in Turkey, although it seems more likely that the Angora known today was first bred in England, well before the 18th century. Although officially protected by law in England, some stock appears to have been exported illegally to France, and thence to other European countries. The distinctive feature of the Angora is its coat, which should be soft, silky and dense. The wool from Angora rabbits is still spun by hand and made into clothing. This breed needs considerable care, however, to ensure that its coat does not become soiled or matted. Regular grooming is essential.

Two distinct forms of Angora now exist. The English variety is characterized by the long clusters of wool at the tips of the ears and on the front feet, which are described as 'furnishings'. The French Angora is a bigger form, with an extremely dense coat that can yield nearly 1kg (2.2lb) of wool a year. Apart from the traditional albino form, the Angora has been bred in various other colours, including silver and blue, as well as golden.

Many Angora owners keep their rabbits in pens with floors of wire mesh, constructed using 16G (gauge) mesh and with individual mesh dimensions of 1.25 x 2.5cm (0.5 x 1in). It is possible to build all-wire cages, but these need to be supported. The individual panels can be fitted together using the special clips sold for linking mesh of this type. The cages can then be held on to a solid wall by brackets.

The Angora has itself contributed to the ancestry of the breed now described as the Swiss Fox, being crossed with a Chinchilla rabbit in the first instance.

Right: **White Swiss Fox**
Descended from the Angora, as shown by its relatively long coat.

Above: **Silver Fawn Angora**
The traditional colour of the Angora is white; this is one of several fine colours that have been bred.

Right: **Sable Angora**
The wool of this breed is highly prized. It is traditionally spun by hand and made into warm cloth.

Argente de Champagne

This silver breed was developed in the Champagne district of France and first described as long ago as 1631. The coloration in this instance is a composite effect: the undercoat is a dark, slatey blue, while the hairs above are bluish white. Longer black hairs are also evident on close inspection of the coat, and together these create an overall impression of silver for the whole animal.

The distinctive coloration is considered a vital feature of the breed for exhibition purposes, and it must be even throughout the coat. Young rabbits of this breed are self black at first. The silver coloration becomes apparent by the age of about two months, but this is a slow process which may not be completed until six months later.

Adults are of medium size, weighing around 3.6kg (8lb), although European stock tends to be slightly heavier than this.

The Argente Bleu is smaller, averaging 2.7kg (6lb) in weight and stockier in overall appearance. While the top coat is unaltered from the Argente de Champagne, the undercoat is lavender, and the long hairs are blue rather than black. The Argente Brun resembles the blue in type, but is brownish in coloration. It is still quite scarce. The smallest and possibly most attractive member of this group is the Argente Creme, with its orange undercoat offset against a creamy pale white body shot with longer orange hairs. Pale white is permitted on the belly in this instance, but a coloured effect is deemed preferable.

Above: **Argente Brun**
A relatively uncommon variety which seems to have originated in France. It was lost for a period before being recreated in the 1940s.

Left: **Argente de Champagne**
Named after the district in France in which it was first developed, its silver coloration is reflected in the word 'Argente'. This is an old breed that dates back to the 17th century.

Below: **Argente Creme**
This is often considered to be the prettiest member of the Argente group. This rabbit is four months old and will not develop its silver coloration fully for several months.

Belgian Hare

In spite of its name, this is a breed of rabbit. The description 'hare' can be traced to its original coloration, but the breed has now become a rich chestnut or tan set against a deep red background. Originally from Belgium, this breed is not as popular as it was in the early years of the 20th century. It is a refined breed, however, a member of the fancy group, and most attractive when in top condition. To maintain their condition, Belgian Hares do require adequate space, however. They reach up to 4kg (9lb) in weight, with ears up to 12.5cm (5in) long.

Since this is a nimble breed with a high stance, be sure to keep it in suitably spacious accommodation.

Beveren

Another Belgian breed, this rabbit is named after the town near Antwerp where it was first kept. The traditional colour is blue, of a light lavender shade, with no trace of silvering in its coat. The first variation from this colour to be developed was the Black in 1919, and during the next decade, the various forms of the white emerged. These are black-eyed, pink-eyed and opal-eyed. A Brown form, which like the other varieties must have even coloration, appeared in the 1930s. The latest development, which occurred during 1980, was the emergence of a lilac Beveren. These attractive but relatively rare rabbits can weigh up to 4.5kg (10lb).

Above: **Belgian Hare**
A descendant of the giant breeds, this rabbit has been developed into an elegant, lithe breed. It will need spacious accommodation to thrive.

Right: **Black and Tan**
This breed arose by chance on an English country estate, being officially recognized in 1891. Related forms include Blue and Tan.

Above: **Deilenaar**
This attractive Dutch breed was developed during the 1940s from the Belgian Hare by crossing with Chinchillas and New Zealand Reds.

Black and Tan
This is the product of pairings involving wild rabbits crossed with members of the Dutch breed, carried out in England towards the end of the 19th century. The Black and Tan has since become quite popular throughout mainland Europe, its markings being considered highly significant for show purposes. Blue, lilac and chocolate colours are now also recognized, all substituting for the black. These rabbits are quite small, weighing about 2kg (4.4lb). The fur should be soft and lie tight against the body, creating a sleek overall appearance. A handsome breed.

Blanc de Bouscat

A white breed that originated in France, the ancestry of the Blanc de Bouscat includes the Flemish Giant and the Angora, as well as the Argente de Champagne. Its fur reflects the Angora ancestry, being at least 3cm (1.2in) long, as well as fine, dense and shiny. The longer white guard hairs contribute to its frosty appearance. The Blanc de Bouscat is indeed a large breed; does weigh up to 6.4kg (14lb), about 1kg (2.2lb) heavier than their mates.

Blanc de Hotot

These relatively scarce rabbits are smaller than the Blanc de Bouscat and do not share a common ancestry. They are white with black eye rings, which should be of even thickness, averaging about 2.5cm (1in) across. These animals have a rather cobby appearance overall. Dwarf and Rex forms have now been developed. A Giant Black variety of this breed was known, but has been lost.

Brun Marron de Lorraine

An attractive but scarce small breed, weighing up to 2kg (4.4lb) with a rounded profile. As its name – Brown Chestnut of Lorraine – suggests, this breed is chestnut-brown in coloration, with yellow underparts. The coat is thick and the eyes are relatively large. It could become very popular as a pet if stock was more widely available.

Californian

This breed was developed in the United States during the early 1920s, in the search for a meat-type rabbit which also had a valuable pelt. The Californian was carefully evolved from Himalayan/Chinchilla crosses, which were then paired to New Zealand Whites. It was officially recognized by the governing American authority, the American Rabbit Breeders Association, during 1939. The Californian is predominantly white, with the characteristic points of the Himalayan still evident, albeit somewhat reduced on the nose. In Britain, both black and milk

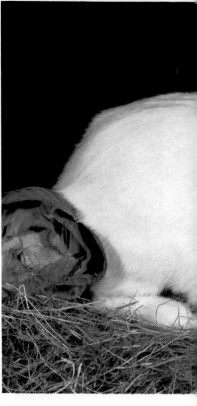

Below: **Blanc de Bouscat**
A popular and prolific French breed developed during the early 1900s. It was intially described as the Ermine.

chocolate points are deemed acceptable, but only the former markings are recognized in the United States. Californians weigh about 4.5kg (10lb).

Above: Blanc de Hotot
Characterized by its black eye rings offset against its pure white coat, this breed has a thickset build.

Below: Californian
The black Himalayan-like points of the Californian are universally recognized in Fancy Rabbit circles.

Chinchilla

The Chinchilla form of the rabbit was evolved in France, from an ancestry which appears to have involved the Himalayan, Blue Beveren and wild rabbits. In colour, these rabbits should resemble the South American Chinchilla, especially popular for its fur during the early part of the 20th century and now widely kept as a pet. The bottom part of the fur close to the skin is therefore a dark slate blue, with a narrower pearl band above, edged with black. The top layer is grey, with black ticking clearly evident. The chest and flanks tend to be slightly paler, being ticked with

pearl. The quality of the fur is a vital feature. It must not be woolly, but needs to be fine, dense, soft to the touch and at least 2.5cm (1in) long.

This breed caused a sensation when it was first seen during 1919 in Britain and the United States and, not surprisingly, other forms have subsequently been developed. Brown, blue and iron-grey variants are now known, while a heavier form described as the American Chinchilla is also seen in the United States. There are two categories: the American Heavy weighs up to about 4.5kg (10lb), whereas bigger rabbits of this type, resulting from crosses involving the Flemish Giant,

were developed in Missouri and can top the scales at nearly 6.8kg (15lb), the does being heavier than the bucks as usual. These are described as the American Giant Chinchillas.

In Britain, a variant known as the Chinchilla Giganta was also evolved from crosses of this type, and tends to be intermediate in size between the two American forms. Slight modifications to the overall type of these rabbits are apparent, most notably in the case of their ears. These are relatively broad at the tips, and create a clear V-shape when the rabbit is looked at head-on as shown in the photograph of this breed on this page.

Cinnamon

The development of rabbit breeds and varieties is a continuing process, and this is one of the most recent results in the United States. It is a combination of cinnamon or rust coloration, with darker markings, forming a butterfly-like outline around the face. Two darker spots are clearly evident on the inner surface of the hindlimbs. Any white toenails are considered a serious fault for exhibition purposes.

Below: **Chinchilla Giganta**
This impressive breed has been developed from crosses involving the Chinchilla and Flemish Giant.

Dutch

One of the most popular and instantly recognizable breeds seen today, the Dutch is derived from Belgian stock, notably the breed known as the Brabancon. These rabbits were developed from animals being exported to England for meat during the late 1800s. One breeder closely scrutinized them as they arrived, seeking a perfectly marked individual showing even areas of black and white fur. He finally obtained one after five years, in 1894, and so began the development of the Dutch rabbit as a fancy breed.

It is difficult to breed a well-marked specimen, which ideally should have a symmetrical inverted V-shaped blaze on its face, with darker markings either side covering the remainder of the head. The front half of the body is white, with a clear delineation leading into a dark area over the rear part. The hind feet, like the forefeet, should be white, however.

Although the traditional patterning is black and white, the Dutch has now been bred in a wide variety of different colours. Blue, chocolate, tortoiseshell and various shades of grey, as well as yellow, are all quite common. For exhibition purposes, the eye colour should match the appropriate standard for the variety concerned.

The Dutch has evolved into a smaller breed than its Belgian ancestor, weighing just over 2kg (4.4lb). As a pet, it is a lively yet compact breed, with bucks often being preferred. While the Dutch itself has grown in popularity, the tricolour Dutch, which appears to be an older breed, has become quite scarce. This is probably because it is difficult to breed specimens conforming to the prescribed exhibition standard. Well-marked individuals show the typical Harlequin markings offset against the characteristics of the Dutch, such as the white blaze on the head.

Right: **Tortoiseshell Dutch**
Clear delineation of markings is a characteristic feature of the breed.

Above: **Tricolour Dutch**
*Bred in a wide variety of colours, the
Dutch is very popular, both as a pet
and on the show bench. This is one
of the early colours.*

Below: **Brown Grey Dutch**
*The contrast between the white and
coloured areas of the fur is
especially pronounced in these
darker individuals of the Dutch.*

English Butterfly

This is another popular breed which has been known for well over a century. Its distinctive markings are a 'butterfly smut', a dark, butterfly-shaped area around the face with 'chain spots' running in a line down the sides of the animal. The ears should be black and the eyes also encircled with an area of black fur. The distribution and size of the spots are vital in a good exhibition specimen, as are the other markings. It is very difficult, therefore, to produce a well-marked individual of this breed.

Apart from the usual black markings, blue, chocolate, tortoiseshell and grey markings are all acceptable in conjunction with white body coloration. It is standard practice to mate a well-marked individual to a so-called 'Charlie', which has only a limited set of markings apparent. This yields better marked youngsters than pairing two well-marked rabbits of this appealing breed.

The English Butterfly is also a popular pet breed, where of course the markings are of little concern.

English Silver

Originally developed for its fur, this breed is now recognized in Europe as the Argente Anglais. Slightly different standards apply, with more varieties recognized under the European standards. Grey, fawn and brown varieties are seen in England, whereas European breeders do not recognize the fawn, but additionally have blue, cream and Havana forms.

Above: **Grey English Silver**
In spite of its name, the coloration in this variety is predominantly black, not grey. It was popular as a fur breed during the last century.

Left: **Blue English Butterfly**
The markings of this particular breed are very important for show purposes. The description of 'butterfly' stems from the distinctive patterning over the nose.

Below: **Fawn English Silver**
The combination of orange and silver in the fur creates an attractive contrast in this appealing breed.

Fée de Marbourg
This is a popular Eastern European breed, derived from the Havana. It is a pale greyish blue with a brown tint, most noticeable on the extremities of the body.

Flemish Giant

This most popular of the surviving giant breeds is likely to weigh over 5kg (11lb). The breed originated in Belgium, around the town of Ghent, where it has traditionally enjoyed a very strong local following. The steel-grey coloration became most popular abroad, notably in the UK and Germany. This colour alone is recognized for show purposes today in the UK, but other countries, including the United States, permit a wider range of colours to be exhibited. The British variety also tends to be slightly smaller and is certainly lighter than its continental counterparts.

These rabbits need to be kept in spacious surroundings and their large size makes them possibly less suitable as pets.

Florida White

Devised specifically for both meat and research purposes, this breed averages around 2.5kg (5.5lb) in weight. It has a cobby shape with a small head, and is a true albino with pure white fur. It was developed from Polish and Dutch stock, with the later addition of New Zealand White blood. As the name suggests, these rabbits were first bred in the State of Florida in the United States.

Right: **White British Giant**
This is a quite separate breed from the English form of the Flemish Giant. Its ancestry is unknown.

Below: **Flemish Giant**
This breed has enjoyed a very loyal following in its Belgian homeland and is now internationally popular.

Harlequin

This breed, originally known as the Japanese, was significantly bigger in the past than it is today. It originated in France and is now relatively scarce, but remains an eye-catching breed. The ideal coat pattern of the Harlequin is based on opposites, one ear being different in colour from the other. Similarly, the head, body and feet are all divided to create contrasts. The basic shades are paired, so that golden orange or fawn is combined with black, blue, lilac and brown coloration. All such combinations are described as Harlequin. In cases where white is consistently present, however, the rabbits are described as Magpies, such as the Lilac Magpie, which is dove grey and white in colour.

Apart from these different combinations, the Harlequin has also been bred in several coat forms. The Rex has a thick, fine and silky coat, like other Rexes, while the Astrex has a curly body coat.

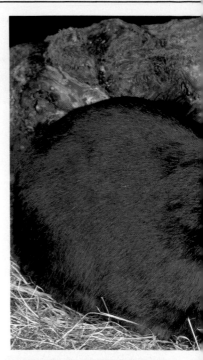

Left: **Havana**
When this breed was first developed, there were two distinctive forms that could be separated by their relative size. A small French variety was also popular for a period. Interestingly, Havanas with relatively sparse coats tend to show the best colour.

Havana

This Dutch mutation appeared at the end of the 19th century. Fur is the most important feature of this breed; it should be of medium length, both dense and glossy, creating a sleek appearance overall. The Havana resembles the Florida White in type, but tends to be slightly heavier. It is a rich chocolate brown, with no white fur or odd hairs apparent in its coat. Older fur does tend to become paler, however, so that during a moult the coat coloration of the Havana appears uneven. A blue form of the Havana has been bred in the United States.

Himalayan

It appears that this breed was developed in the Far East, possibly in China, and was introduced to European rabbit fanciers during the 19th century. As with other livestock where the Himalayan gene has emerged, such as cats, the depth of coloration on the extremities of the body (known as the 'points') is influenced markedly by the local environmental temperature. It tends to darken as the air temperature decreases. The remainder of the body is white and the eyes are pinkish in colour.

Although the points of nose, ears, feet and tail are traditionally black, other point coloration is also recognized, including blue, lilac and chocolate. The show standard for the Himalayan tends to vary slightly, however, depending upon the country concerned. Although superficially similar to the Californian, the Himalayan is significantly smaller, weighing only about 2.5kg (5.5lb). These rabbits seem naturally tame, do not resent handling, and so make an ideal choice as a pet.

Above: **Himalayan Rex**
The Himalayan is a popular pet because of its friendly nature. The young tend to appear greyish at first, but gradually change colour.

Left: **Black Harlequin**
A rabbit of distinct contrasts, this variety has a pattern of deep black, offset against golden orange. Those with white are known as Magpies.

71

Lilac

There is dispute over the ancestry of this breed, but it is closely related to the Havana. It may have emerged spontaneously in a litter of Havanas, or it could be the result of mating with a blue Beveren, the offspring then being paired together to yield a proportion of lilac offspring. It still shows a resemblance to the Havana in terms of type. The Lilac has a pinkish dove coloration, evenly distributed throughout the coat. It was known by 1910, although the 'Gouenaar' (Gouda), a Dutch breed with a similar coat coloration, had been developed previously.

Lop breeds

The unmistakable appearance of these rabbits stems from their ears, which hang down, rather than being held erect.

The English Lop, the oldest of the breeds, was known by the early years of the 19th century. Such rabbits became exceedingly popular, the ears being especially significant in exhibition Lops. Apart from the actual carriage, their length, width and overall shape are all judged. The ear's length is measured from behind with a wooden ruler: by four months of age, the ears may be over 60cm (24in) in overall length. Width is measured at the broadest part of the ear. Body coloration is generally considered of limited significance compared with the ears of this breed. Patterned individuals should display a noticeable butterfly smut, which should be in contrast if the surrounding is white. Sooty fawn is a popular coloration.

The French Lop is a massive and thickset breed, with a well-muscled body. The top of the head should form a distinctive crown, surrounded by the ears, which hang down close to the cheeks, obscuring the ear canals. The natural agouti coloration is most

Above: **Lilac**
A close relative of the Havana, the Lilac should have an even depth of coloration throughout its coat.

Right: **Sooty Fawn English Lop**
This photograph shows the impressive size of the ears. Take care to protect them from injury.

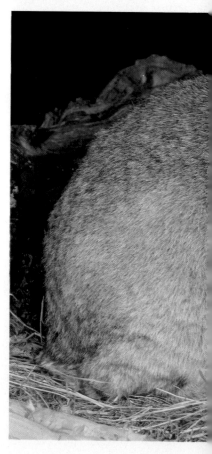

Right: **Agouti French Lop**
Lop rabbits are characterized by the carriage of their ears. The French variety has a prominent crown with its ears forming a horseshoe shape.

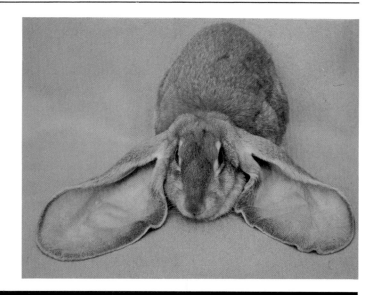

commonly associated with this breed, while the coat itself should be dense.

The Dwarf Lop is virtually identical to the French breed, but is significantly smaller and lighter. It should be about half the usual weight of the French, which averages around 4.5kg (10lb). Shoulder spots, present on both sides of the body, are permitted in this breed. It seems likely that crossings involving Dutch rabbits gave rise to this miniature breed.

Right: **Meissner Lop**
A German breed reflecting the silver ancestry in its coat. The silvering should extend forward to the head, as clearly shown in this individual. A relatively small breed among Lops.

The Meissner Lop, similar to the English in some respects, was developed in Germany and is a finer type overall than the French Lop. It was produced by pairings involving silvered rabbits, and a wide variety of colours are recognized, the coats being evenly silvered. The ears should be at least 38cm (15in) in length, and can be nearly 5cm (2in) longer. The ears are similar in carriage to the French Lop, reflecting the influence of this breed.

Of all these breeds, the Dwarf form is probably the most suitable for a pet, being more easily managed and possibly less likely to injure its pendulous ears. Take particular care with these rabbits to ensure that there are no loose ends of wire or nails in the hutch or cage.

Above: **Sooty Dwarf Lop**
While the Agouti form is still the most common, breeders have now produced Lops in a wide range.

Left: **Sooty Butterfly Dwarf Lop**
Dwarf Lops are ideal for anyone who wishes to keep these distinctive rabbits but is limited by space.

Right: **Cashmere Lop**
This fluffy new breed is becoming popular. It appears to have been bred at least in part from the Angora.

Netherland Dwarf

This miniature breed is derived from crossings of the Dutch and Polish rabbits. A relatively recent development in the rabbit fancy, the Netherland Dwarf has gained an international following in a short space of time. It was bred initially during the late 1940s and reached North America only in 1969. The original stock was hampered by breeding problems, and suffered a high incidence of dental malocclusion, but these difficulties have now been overcome to a great extent. These rabbits should be cobby overall, with short front legs and slightly rounded ears just 5cm (2in) in length. Their fur should be both soft and dense. A mark of quality is seen when the fur is brushed against the natural lie of the coat and slowly realigns itself.

Apart from its distinctive size, weighing only 1kg (2.2lb), the Netherland Dwarf has been bred in a vast array of colours and patterns, covering virtually all the possible combinations recognized in rabbits. Indeed, so numerous are the varieties that they are arranged in distinct groups. The selfs comprise pure colours, such as white, whereas the shaded and agouti patterned are colour combinations, as in the Chinchilla variety. Another group contains those rabbits with a tan patterning, while a fifth group features varieties not included elsewhere, such as the Himalayan Netherland Dwarf. This breed offers considerable scope, therefore, to either the pet seeker or exhibition breeder, but in the latter case, specialization is recommended.

Below:
Black Otter Netherland Dwarf
A striking colour in one of the most popular breeds available today.

Below:
Marten Smoke Netherland Dwarf
Ideal as compact pets, but some Netherland Dwarfs may be nervous.

Above: **Agouti Netherland Dwarf**
The Netherland Dwarf is descended from Polish stock crossed with Dutch rabbits during the 1940s.

New Zealand breeds

The New Zealand White is the most popular of these breeds. The New Zealand Red and Black breeds were developed in the United States, while a New Zealand Blue has been developed in the United Kingdom.

The White is a versatile breed which, because of its rapid growth rate, is also popular for meat. It is a true albino, with pink eyes. While dense, the coat tends to be rather coarse, as in related breeds.

The New Zealand Red is the original breed in this category, having been developed during the early years of the 20th century from an ancestry which probably included Belgian Hares and Golden Fawn rabbits. The standard for this breed is again variable; British judges seek a slightly smaller rabbit and a more golden coloration than their United States counterparts. The combination of the white and red forms gave rise to the New Zealand Black, which was officially recognized in 1958. Again, there are slight variations for judging purposes, but the coloration should be jet black overall, apart from the eyes, which are brown, and the toenails, which must be dark blue.

Palomino

This breed was developed in the United States in about 1952. There are two recognized forms of the Palomino: the Golden and the Lynx. The Golden has a cream undercoat and light gold guard hairs extending through the coat. Circles around the eyes and the underparts are paler, merging with the gold coloration on the lower flanks. The claws must be dark. In the Palomino Lynx, the coat is basically orange, with a white undercoat. The fur should be tipped evenly and lightly with lilac, creating a silvery sheen. It can be difficult to establish the right amount of ticking for this purpose. The eyes, as in the Golden Palomino, should be either hazel or brown. These rabbits weigh about 4kg (8.8lb), with does heavier.

Right: **New Zealand White**
This rabbit is a true albino with no pigment, as shown by its pink eyes.

Giant Papillon

Also known as the French Butterfly, this breed shows the typical butterfly patterning, known as the 'smut' across its nose. It is most widely kept in mainland Europe, having originated in France. The coat is essentially white. Apart from darker markings on the head and ears, there is an area of colour running along the back, with some spots present on the flanks. Black markings are most common, but there are no restrictions on colour.

Right: **New Zealand Red**
This attractive rabbit clearly has Belgian Hare ancestry. It produces large litters of up to eight young.

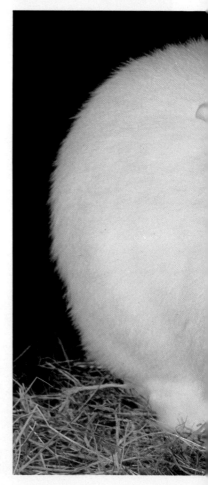

Polish

An old breed, the Polish is known as the 'Britannia petite' in North America. It shows a close affinity with the Netherland Dwarf, reflecting the ancestral link between these two breeds. The Polish is an albino and now considerably smaller than formerly, weighing just over 1kg (2.2lb) at most. Its stance is characteristic of the breed, with head held high and ears erect, almost touching each other. The maximum length for the ears is set at 6.35cm (2.5in). The eyes should be bold and deep red, although a blue-eyed form is also recognized for show purposes. The coat is pure white in colour.

A slightly different breed has evolved in the United States, where it is known as the American Polish Rabbit, while varieties with other colours appear to be currently gaining in popularity. In spite of its small size, this is a lively breed, although reasonably easy to handle.

Above: **Marten Smoke Polish**
A particularly attractive colour variety of this lively small breed. The ears are short and held erect.

Below: **Orange Polish**
This is still a young rabbit and the depth of its coat coloration is not yet developed to its full extent.

Above: **Ermine Rex**
The Rex mutation affects the texture of the coat, producing a velvety fur. The Ermine Rex is pure white.

Below: **Havana Rex**
Coarse guard hairs are reduced in the coat of Rexes, helping to emphasize the sleek body outline.

Rexes

These distinctive rabbits are characterized by the velvety texture and appearance of their fur. In this instance, the hairs of the coat and the guard hairs, which are usually longer, are of the same length, effectively blending together. Another distinctive feature is the appearance of the whiskers, which are relatively short and curled. Rexes have been known in the rabbit fancy for many years, but only in 1919 in France was there a serious attempt to develop these unusual features into a new breed. The coat length should be at least 1.25cm (0.5in), with longer fur approaching 2cm (0.8in) overall being required in mainland European show stock.

The Rex is divided into similar categories as the Netherland Dwarf. Among self Rexes, the Black is one of the most popular, and now shows less of a tendency to a relatively thin coat. Any trace of white is considered a serious fault, and the coat must be in top condition for an exhibition. The Ermine Rex is another striking variety in this

category, and should be pure white, with no trace of yellow evident in the fur. The coat again needs to be dense, silky and exhibit a good sheen. One of the more unusual colours is the Orange Rex, derived from the New Zealand Red. In the United States, this variety lacks any white markings on the belly and is known as the Red Rex.

It can be difficult to breed certain varieties of Rex, including the Chinchilla Rex, or 'Chinrex' as it is occasionally described.

Assessment of the coat quality in these animals needs to be deferred, as in other such cases, until the young rabbit first moults. Until then, this particular variety frequently has guard hairs still present in its coat that create a coarse appearance. These disappear with maturity.

Always check the legs of a Rex rabbit to ensure that it is not devoid of fur on the hocks, as this is classed as an exhibition fault. If it has been kept on a hard floor with little bedding, the animal may have rubbed the hairs off in some cases.

Rex rabbits offer considerable scope for exhibition, with a wide choice of varieties available. They are easy to maintain, provided they are given an adequate layer of bedding in their quarters.

Rhinelander

A German breed, the Rhinelander shows the English Butterfly in its ancestry in the typical dark patterning across the nostrils. It has a saddle marking along its back, and between six and eight spots on each side of the flanks. These rabbits are seen most commonly in mainland Europe, and are instantly recognized by their triple coloration. The basic body is white, with a combination of yellow and black markings. No overlap must occur between these latter shades.

Sables

The Sable is divided into the Marten and Siamese types, with three shades recognized in each type, from dark through medium to light. The early Sables were produced from pairings involving Chinchillas and were discarded at first. Certainly, they were of poor quality compared with those seen today. As a fur breed, their coats tended to be thin and poor in colour.

Below: **Rhinelander**
Characterized by their unusual tricoloured appearance, perfect Rhinelanders are hard to breed.

Above: **Orange Rex**
Considered by some to be the most striking of all the Rexes, the Orange is indeed a most attractive variety.

The Marten Sable was the first form to be developed. This variety should be sepia overall, of the appropriate shade, being mixed on the flanks and lower parts with longer white hairs. A different show classification is applied to these rabbits in the United States, where this variety is described as the Silver Marten Sable; the English version is recognized separately, being grouped alongside the English Silver Fox.

The Siamese is identical to the Marten in type, weighing about 3.2kg (7lb) and differing only in terms of colour. The tan patterning of the Marten is whitish in this instance, the quality of the coat remaining vital. Since the dark form closely resembles a self, the description 'Siamese' is confined to the light and medium shades in the United States.

A dilute form of the Sable, the Smoke Pearl, is also known, having first been bred in about 1920. The coloration in this variety is a combination of beige and pale pearl grey, giving a smoke effect that extends over the full length of the back, becoming more beige on the sides of the body.

Satin

This breed arose in a litter of Havanas during the 1930s, and has since become very popular because of its glossy smooth satin coat. Particular emphasis is placed on this feature in exhibition Satin rabbits. The satin characteristic has now been combined with a large variety of colours, as in the case of the Rex mutations. Satins tend to be cobby in appearance, with short necks, and of medium size with weights about 3.2kg (7lb). The coat should be about 2.5cm (1in) long, but its overall appearance in terms of density, texture and sheen is more important than its length.

Siberian

Two forms of this breed are known, of which the original type is now considered to be extinct. The modern Siberian dates from 1930, and was originally brown, although other colours are now acceptable, notably blue, black and lilac. The fur is thick and has an obvious sheen. Ticking is a serious fault in exhibition stock, as are any areas of white fur.

Silver Fox

This is a European breed, not to be confused with the American Silver Fox, which has an even distribution of white hairs over its whole coat. These markings are restricted to the

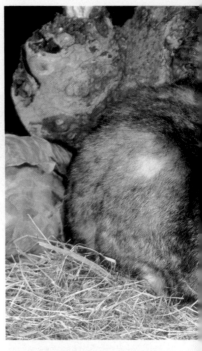

Below: **Black Silver Fox**
The origin of this breed of rabbit can be traced back to the 1920s. It was developed to resemble the Canadian Silver Fox, after which it was named, in terms of its coat type and colour. It has been produced in a variety of other colours.

Above: **Castor Satin**
Satin rabbits are of American origin, but like the Rex, this is a mutation affecting the coat. It has in turn been combined with many colours.

lower parts in the Silver Fox itself, and this breed is significantly lighter, not exceeding 3.2kg (7lb).

Silver Marten
This is an American combination of the Chinchilla and the Black and Tan. As with the English Silver Fox, the Silver Marten occurs in blue, chocolate, lilac and black.

Thuringer
This German breed is known in its homeland as the Chamois de Thuringe. These rabbits weigh about 4kg (8.8lb) and their coat has thick, short fur which is buff, with darker guard hairs. Bluish black areas should be apparent on the sides of the body and on the points, also extending to the underparts. The head is relatively broad, while the neck is short, emphasizing the compact shape of the breed. These rabbits are considered dual-purpose, for fur and fancy.

Viennas
There are three colour forms of the Vienna, a breed which is popular on the European mainland. The first is a dark slate blue, with a stocky and well-muscled body. The coat itself is both dense and silky. Known to have been in existence by the end of the 19th century, the variety is believed to have originated in Austria, but this is disputed. The White Vienna tends to be smaller than its Blue counterpart, and should be pure white in colour. These are reputed to be hardy rabbits, popular in eastern parts of Europe. The third member of the group is the Grey Vienna, which was bred in Germany. This is bluish grey at the base of its fur, with various forms of grey above (including the colour of the wild form, described as agouti) being acceptable for show purposes. These breeds weigh between 4-5kg (8.8-11lb), the correct weight being a significant feature in the show standard.

Guinea pigs

The guinea pig was probably first seen in Europe during the 1500s, being brought back from South America by the Spaniards. In spite of originating in a tropical area, these rodents proved hardy in temperate climates. They were soon breeding freely and became increasingly popular as pets. Today, exhibition breeders try to produce guinea pigs that conform as closely as possible to the standards laid down for each variety. Breeding these rodents is usually straightforward.

Breeding

Guinea pigs are generally mature at about three months of age, but ideally should not be used for breeding until they are four or five months old. After this time, however, the hip bones become more tightly fused, and if the sow has not already had a litter, the slight likelihood of birth difficulties (known as dystocia) is probably increased.

These birth difficulties will require immediate veterinary attention if suspected.

The female's oestrus cycle lasts about sixteen days on average, and the sow can be left with the boar for several weeks to ensure that mating takes place. If required, a boar can cover a harem of four sows at a time. The average gestation period is about sixty-three days, although this will not be easy to calculate unless the date of mating is known with certainty. The young may be born as early as fifty-nine days after mating, but if the gestation period extends beyond seventy-two days, it is likely that the litter will be born dead. There can be a relatively high incidence of dead offspring in guinea pigs, especially at and immediately after birth.

Following a month of sharing the boar's accommodation (or a shorter period if mating is observed), transfer the sow back to her own hutch to have her litter. She will

become very heavy as birth approaches, and if possible should not be handled during this phase, since this may harm her offspring. The average litter consists of about four youngsters, although as many as ten are not unknown. They are born fully developed, with their eyes open and a full covering of hair. Although they may use their teeth to start feeding when only a day or so old, young guinea pigs will not be independent until about one month of age. Assuming that suitable foster parents are available, it may be best to divide up a large litter for, perhaps surprisingly, the sow has only two nipples for all her offspring.

Immediately before giving birth, the sow is at risk from the ailment known as pregnancy toxaemia, especially if she is fat. This is a metabolic disorder which can rapidly prove fatal. Loss of appetite and signs of severe muscular twitching are most common indicators. Prompt veterinary treatment can often reverse these symptoms successfully, however. Maintaining a regular supply of greenfood will help to minimize the risk of this condition appearing. Another problem encountered in albino guinea pigs at this stage is hair loss. This becomes worse with successive litters, but generally the hair will regrow within a month.

Like many other rodents, the sow guinea pig will be able to mate successfully within hours of giving birth, but this should not be encouraged. Guinea pigs can breed until late in life, but most sows will have ceased by the time they are three years old, although boars are likely to remain fertile for longer.

Below: *A 'pet' guinea pig of the type widely available in pet stores. As the following pages show, selective breeding throughout the world has led to the development of a wide range of colours combined with a number of different coat types.*

Colour and coat types

Guinea pigs have now been developed in a large number of varieties affecting both coat and colour, but basically there are three major coat types available: smooth-coated, Abyssinian and Peruvian. Selection of the coat type should be a foremost consideration since the Peruvian has a long, trailing coat that needs considerable grooming if the hairs are not to become matted and unsightly. The coat also grows fast, as much as 2.5cm (1in) in a month. (See also page 102.)

The major varieties of guinea pig are described below. As with rabbits, each must conform to the prescribed standard as closely as possible if being exhibited. In this context, there are two broad divisions: the so-called Self Varieties feature all the smooth-coated guinea pigs of a single colour; the Non-Self Category of guinea pigs covers all other varieties and coat types.

Self varieties

Self guinea pigs are of a single colour only, but in this context the term also describes the variety itself, which is short-haired. Other self-coloured guinea pigs, such as Abyssinians, are therefore not included in Self classes at shows.

Type is considered an important feature of these guinea pigs. They should have a broad head with a relatively short face, and bold, bright eyes. The petal-shaped ears should droop and must obviously be

undamaged, showing no signs of a slight tear for example. It can be difficult to assess type as well as colour in young guinea pigs before they mature. Their bodies may seem rather long compared with the desirable shape, which is cobby.

The coat itself should be relatively fine and, partly for this reason, sows are often preferred for exhibition purposes. Their heads also tend to be better shaped.

While the smooth-coated pet guinea pig needs no grooming, this process is an important part of the show preparation for an exhibition cavy. Grooming is essentially by hand, some exhibitors preferring to rub a piece of silk along the natural lie of the fur to impart a final 'gloss' to their entry's coat.

Self Black

A deep, glossy black, this variety is especially striking and has proved one of the most popular members of this group. Some specimens may be spoilt by having odd reddish hairs, however, while white markings are another serious blemish. Self Blacks must also have a matching undercoat.

Below: **Self Black (Crested)**
The Self Black is one of the most popular of the Self varieties, but it can be difficult to produce a good specimen free from any trace of reddish or white hairs. Young guinea pigs of this colour may loose some, if not all, of their reddish tint as they mature, however, This is a Crested specimen – see page 104.

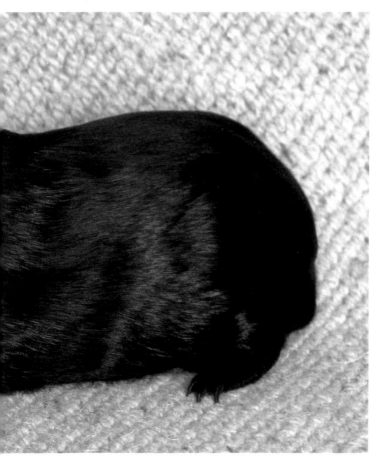

Self White

The pure albino form of this variety is characterized by its red eyes. There is also a dark-eyed variety, however, which often retains some pigment so that its ears, especially, may be dark. The Dark-eyed White presents a greater challenge for exhibition purposes, since although pigmentation on the body and feet may be removed by selective breeding, eye coloration often suffers accordingly. The type of this variety also tends to be less satisfactory than its red-eyed counterpart, notably in terms of head shape.

As with other pale-coated breeds, coloration needs to be pure. It is vital to keep these animals under spotless conditions to minimize the risk of dirty marks on their fur. In older individuals of both forms, the fur can become yellowish.

Above: **Dark-eyed Self Golden**
This form is relatively scarce compared with its pink-eyed counterpart, but equally attractive.

Below: **Self Cream; Buff; Golden**
The depth of coloration of these attractive self colours can be variable. Self Cream shown at left.

Above: **Pink-eyed Self Golden**
Young Goldens tend to be deeper in colour than adults. A white-collared form has also been bred.

Self Cream

The coloration in this variety is highly significant. The shade of cream must be neither too dark nor too light, and should show no trace of yellow. Within any litter there will be a natural variety of colour and the paler shades are preferred. The undercoat should correspond to the coat colour, while the eyes are ruby red. A very attractive combination.

Self Golden

The depth of coloration can vary considerably between individuals of this variety, ranging from a shade of brass to a virtual red. The ideal lies midway between these extremes and, as always, the undercoat is very important in creating the correct impression. A rich golden, sometimes described as ginger, the undercoat must match the colour of the top coat. The eyes are pink, although there is also a dark-eyed form which, as in the case of the Self White, tends to be harder to breed without losing eye colour along with unwanted skin pigmentation.

Self Chocolate

Coloration in this instance should be dark rather than pale. The eyes should also be dark brown, as well as the ears. It can be difficult to obtain the desired depth of coloration, however. The underparts are sometimes paler, with odd white hairs visible, and this is a serious fault in exhibition stock.

Self Red

This variety has declined to some extent, with quality stock now growing quite scarce. The colour should be a dark, rich mahogany red, with matching ears and feet. The eyes are deep ruby. Young guinea pigs of this variety will become lighter as they grow older, so the darkest individuals should be kept for exhibition purposes, assuming that their type is adequate. A few white hairs in a young Self Red need not necessarily cause concern. These may well be replaced, leaving solid coloration, and some breeders claim that individuals showing a trace of white produce offspring with the best coloration. The change to solid coloration may not be apparent until six months of age.

Self Beige

The Self Beige is a diluted form of Chocolate, with pink eyes. The standard tends to give relatively little guidance on the precise coloration required, although a medium shade is deemed preferable. Uneven coloration is unfortunately often a feature of this variety, however. Members of a litter are likely to differ quite noticeably in coloration, and the tendency is to pair opposites together in the hope of obtaining medium-shaded offspring. Type in this instance tends to be less good than in other Selfs, but continuing efforts are being made by committed breeders in this direction.

Below: **Self Chocolate**
These guinea pigs invariably have very soft coats. The coloration should be even and dark, resembling plain chocolate.

Above: **Self Red**
This is an impressive member of the Self group, but good specimens can be hard to obtain. The standard calls for a deep shade of red, resembling mahogany and free from any white markings. The rich coloration is emphasized by the glossy coat, offset against ears of a matching colour. Ruby red eyes.

Above: **Self Beige**
Note how the coloration of these four-day old babies is darker than that of their mother. The Beige is the dilute form of the Chocolate; thus the eyes are pink, as are the ears. Avoid individuals with uneven depth of coloration for showing, as this is considered a bad fault. Pairing opposites may get good results.

Self Lilac

There is a similarity between the Self Lilac and the Self Beige, but the former should be a medium shade of dove grey, without any trace of beige in its coat. It is in fact the dilute form of the Self Black, and again should have pink eyes. Coloration tends to fade as young guinea pigs of this variety mature, as also occurs in the case of the Beige.

Other Selfs

In the United States, certain Selfs not recognized in the UK are included in show schedules. Among these is the Self Blue, which should be of a dark, rich shade and must

have matching eyes. The Red-eyed Orange may be another American variety less well known to the British fancier, but does in fact correspond to the Self Golden recognized in the UK. As its name suggests, its coat is reddish orange; it is darker in young animals. New Selfs include the Buff, which is a dark shade of Cream.

Below: **Self Lilac**
This is the dilute form of the Self Black. The ideal coloration is considered to be dove grey with a pinkish overlay. The coat texture in this variety is often rather coarse, so that these guinea pigs are often groomed carefully before a show. The eye colour is usually pink.

Non-Self Varieties

The varieties in this section can be short-haired and not self-coloured, or they can show different coat characteristics, in which case they can be self-coloured.

Abyssinians

Examples of this breed are widely kept as both pets and exhibition subjects. Their coat consists of a mixture of rosettes and ridges, the hair which grows outwards to form one rosette creating a ridge when it meets the hair of an adjacent rosette. The number of rosettes is crucial for show purposes. There should be four rosettes extending over the saddle region in a straight line, and four around the rump, while up to two must be present on each shoulder. The distribution of these rosettes is also critical if the ridges are to run in a straight line, as is desirable. The shape of the individual rosettes is similarly important. They must have a tiny, clearly defined middle, and be well developed. Nowhere on the body should the fur be flat, which can be suggestive of a long coat. In reality, this is not the case, since the maximum length of the hair at any point should be 3.8cm (1.5in) only.

Below: *The various rosettes of the Abyssinian guinea pig are an important feature of this breed, particularly for exhibition stock.*

Understandably, therefore, it is not easy to produce an Abyssinian with a coat perfect in every detail. Colour is not considered a significant feature, but white Abyssinians are generally unpopular since their coats are not sufficiently harsh to stand away from the body and tend to lack vigour. Because all Self Abyssinians have quite soft coats, Tortoiseshells, Roans and Brindle varieties tend to be popular for show purposes because they are of better type and have coarser coats.

The Tortoiseshell should be red and black, with no overlap of these shades where they meet in the coat. This also applies to the Tortoiseshell and White form. The Brindle is described as 'light' if its coat displays red rather than black hairs, and 'heavily brindled' if the situation is reversed.

There is also a category called Off-colours, Any Other Variety (A.O.V.) or Any Other Colour (A.O.C.), featuring varieties not included under other headings for this breed. Among these are the Red and White combination, as well as the Agoutis and Himalayans.

Show preparation is important for Abyssinians. A toothbrush makes a useful, suitably sized grooming tool. Choose one with natural bristles if possible, to reduce the likelihood of static charges that will inhibit the natural 'lie' of the coat. Giving the

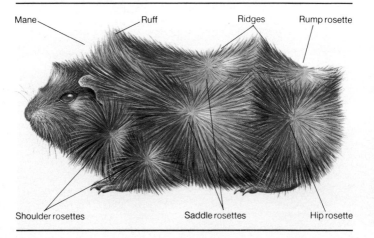

Mane — Ruff — Ridges — Rump rosette

Shoulder rosettes — Saddle rosettes — Hip rosette

animals an occasional bath is also recommended by some exhibitors.

The Abyssinian boar has gained a relatively bad reputation for aggression towards its fellows, but this is certainly not always justified. These animals need regular and careful handling from an early age, however, to prevent them becoming nervous in later life.

Top: **Brindle Abyssinian**
Colour in the case of this breed is not considered significant in show circles, but the coarser coat texture of some varieties is often favoured.

Above:
Tortie and White Abyssinian
The colours should be well defined for exhibition, as shown here.

Agoutis

The typical ticked appearance of the Agoutis results from two distinct shades existing on each hair, thereby creating a banded effect linked with plain colours. The two best-known varieties are the Golden Agouti and the Silver Agouti. The former has golden ticking, with a significantly darker base to its hairs, while the underparts have a more reddish tinge. The Silver Agouti has a bluish black coloration underneath, tipped with silver, becoming darker on the belly.

Other types of Agouti are known, including a cinnamon form in which the silver tipping is topped by a light shade of chocolate brown. In addition, both Lemon and Orange Agoutis are occasionally seen. These can be distinguished because the Orange has a brown, rather than black, base to its hairs.

By using Dilute (i.e. pale) forms, such as the Lilac, it is possible to breed corresponding Agoutis with red eyes. These are often described as Argentes. The diluting effect restricts the impact of the ticking,

however, so that these animals are not very striking. An Agouti may be penalized at a show for having 'bonnet strings', or a light band of fur, where even ticking is required.

Dutch

These smooth-coated guinea pigs have white fur augmented by colour. The pattern of markings required is similar to that for rabbits of the Dutch breed, and all forms can be successfully bred in guinea pigs. There should again be very clear delineation between the bands of shaded hair and the central circular band of white. The whole appearance of these animals must be balanced, including the white blaze marking on the nose, which should extend up to the forehead between the ears.

It is very difficult to breed the perfectly marked Dutch guinea pig, and in this instance coloration is also considered significant in breeding stock. Cream is not a shade commonly associated with the Dutch, however, because it becomes pale on the belly and no clear boundary then exists between the cream and white areas. The Black and the Red, the typical forms of the Dutch, can create a most attractive appearance in a well-marked individual, but Agoutis are also not unknown.

Left: Golden and Silver Agoutis
The baby Golden Agouti at left shows the typical darker coat compared to the adult Silver alongside. Both have the distinctive ticking pattern seen in all Agoutis.

Left: Silver Agouti Coronet
The Agouti feature, with both light and dark hairs present in the coat, can also be introduced to the long-haired forms of the guinea pig, as shown by this handsome specimen.

Above: **Dutch and White Rex**
This Dutch Rex female, shown here with her White Rex offspring, displays the typical white facial blaze. The markings should resemble those in Dutch rabbits.

Tortoiseshell and White

This guinea pig has areas of white, black and red fur on its body. The pattern of markings is extremely demanding. Even shaped squares should form a patchwork on both sides of the body, with clear straight lines of demarcation visible where the different shades join together. It seems almost impossible to predict the likely pattern of markings from any given pair, even if they are well marked themselves. In view of this inconsistency, the variety can be a frustrating one to breed. In a truly well-marked specimen, the colour must also be deep, otherwise it will be penalized.

'Tortie and White' guinea pigs, as they are popularly known, can be exhibited without perfect markings because the standard for this variety is so demanding, but they will be heavily penalized for the absence of a particular coloration. If this problem is confined to one side of the body, it can help to mate the faulty guinea pig to an individual with an excess of that particular colour in the same area. This may compensate for the problem in the next generation.

Himalayan

The Himalayan guinea pig, like its rabbit counterpart, has a white body with darker points, which should be either black or chocolate. It can be difficult to distinguish between the two shades, since the black is equivalent to a dark, plain chocolate, whereas the chocolate is paler. While depth of coloration at the points can again vary, depending on temperature, the ears are perhaps the most reliable means of separating the two shades.

Serious breeders of Himalayans take considerable trouble to ensure that their guinea pigs have points of good colour. To achieve this, keep them out of a run during the summer, when the sun is likely to be hottest, since this will cause the points to fade. A cool outhouse is the best option, or a hutch in a

shaded spot if they are being kept out of doors.

Young Himalayans will not develop their full colour until they are about six months old. They are born pure white and the points emerge gradually as they get older, the pads being the first of the points to turn dark in colour.

Above: **Himalayan**
The Black Himalayan youngster (left) shows darker points than the Chocolate (Crested) alongside.

Below: **Tortoiseshell and White**
This superb guinea pig shows the characteristic combination of red, black and white of the variety.

Peruvian

This breed never fails to attract attention at exhibitions. It is not really entirely suitable as a pet, however, unless you can spend long periods each day grooming its distinctive coat. The long hair should stem from just two rosettes on the rump; any rosettes on the back itself will be a crucial handicap for show purposes. If you do not wish to show your Peruvian, the coat can of course be clipped regularly. Indeed, breeding stock is generally maintained in this way.

The Peruvian is born with a relatively short coat. Only at around three months will its hair begin to be trained for exhibition. Then a so-called 'wrapper' of paper, stabilized with balsa wood, is used to hold the 'sweep' of hair which trails down from the rosettes. Some guinea pigs may not be persuaded to leave their wrappers in place, especially when side wrappers are added at around six months of age. Handling is very important from an early age, to encourage the guinea pig to remain still when required. This is because

Peruvians are judged on a raised showstand approximately 15cm (6in) high and 45cm (18in) square, covered with hessian sacking. It is easy to make such a stand for training purposes.

The Peruvian is therefore a breed for the dedicated specialist. Indeed, the whole of its management is geared to maximizing the appearance of its coat for show purposes. Animals must be kept on their own and their hutches should be lined with hay provided in a hay rack. The bedding will not then become entangled in the profuse coat, which in a good specimen can be 50cm (20in) in total length.

Below: *Preparing a Peruvian guinea pig for showing involves wrapping the long trailing coat as shown here to keep it in top condition. Use strips of brown paper 15cm (6in) wide and balsa wood blocks measuring 5x2.5cm (2x1in). At first, use one wrapper on the sweep, or tail end, plus one on each side. As the coat grows, enlarge the wrappers and use more of them as necessary.*

Wrapping a Peruvian

1 Position balsa block on paper

2 Fold over and secure with tape

3 Fold sides of paper over centre panel

4 Fold up in a concertina shape

5 Unfold and place under hair

6 Refold and secure with a rubber band

Peruvians unfortunately show an abnormal tendency to chew their own coats, which can ruin the potential of a show specimen very rapidly. A constant supply of hay may help to prevent this habit. Parasitic or skin disease of any kind can also prove a serious problem.

Below: This photograph shows how the coat of the Peruvian guinea pig has evolved in just over a century. The preserved specimen in the glass case shown at top dates from 1880 and the coat is clearly different in style from that of the modern Peruvian shown in front of it.

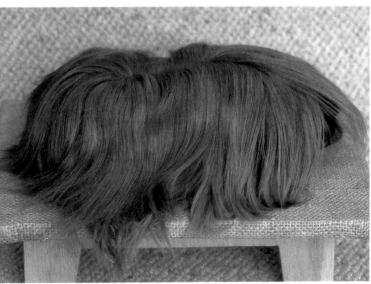

Above: **Slate Peruvian**
This fine specimen is displayed on a show stand, which is typically 15cm (6in) high and covered with hessian.

The stand allows the flowing coat to be seen to best advantage. It is vital to 'train' such breeds from an early age so that they remain still.

103

Sheltie
This breed is similar to the Peruvian, but whereas the Peruvian with its characteristic rosettes is the long-haired counterpart of the Abyssinian, the Sheltie is the equivalent variety of the Self group. Shelties tend to be less common than Peruvians, but their management is similar. Again, colour is not considered a significant feature.

Crested
The Crested guinea pig was first bred in the United States, and introduced to the UK from Canada in 1972. The Crest is actually a rosette, the middle of which is located slightly in front of the ears and above the eyes. Breeders in the United States have aimed to produce guinea pigs with crests of a different colour from that of the main body, whereas the English Crested

Above: **Tricolour Sheltie**
This attractive breed is also known as the 'Silky' in the United States. Although at first glance its coat is similar to that of the Peruvian, it can be distinguished because the long hair does not extend over the head.

Right:
Himalayan Chocolate Crested
The Crested mutation is still being developed to its full potential. In the USA, the trend is to produce individuals with a crest colour different to that of the body. In the English Crested, it is the same.

is a true self. Experimental breeding is leading to the combination of the crested characteristic with other varieties, such as the Himalayan, Dutch and Sheltie. This trend is likely to continue, with breeders then refining the type of the offspring for exhibition purposes.

Roan

The characteristic of this variety is a combination of self and white hair, evenly distributed through the coat. The so-called Strawberry Roan, for example, is a combination of red and white. Black and white Roans are also popular. Roans should not be paired with each other, however, because a genetic problem of blindness affects white offspring in their litters. Instead, a Roan is paired with its self counterpart. The heads of Roans, as well as their feet, should ideally reflect their pure self ancestry, i.e. matching in colour.

Dalmatian

This is one of the more popular new varieties, with a spotted coat as its name suggests. The head tends to be solid in colour, with a white central blaze. The spots themselves are usually black or greyish, although a chocolate form of the Dalmatian has now been developed. As with the Roan, Dalmatians must not be paired together.

Right: **Blue Roan**
Roans differ quite considerably in appearance. The Blue shown here has fairly even coloration, whereas in the Dappled Roan the pattern is uneven, as its name suggests. Strawberry Roans are also bred.

Below: **Dalmation**
The Dalmatian mutation, named after the similar breed of dog, is a relatively recent development in guinea pig circles. The solid colour takes the form of small spots, similar to peas in size and shape.

Rex (Teddy)

The Rex mutation in the guinea pig is of relatively recent origin, first appearing in stock kept at a school in Yorkshire, England. An identical form has also arisen in Canada, and it is now described as the Teddy throughout North America. There are no guard hairs in the coat, causing it to appear wavy at first and then woolly in older guinea pigs.

Tortoiseshell

Although an old form, this has never become very popular. It resembles the Tortoiseshell and White, but lacks the white coloration, and is still regarded as a rare variety in show circles. Part of the problem is that it appears impossible to breed a guinea pig of this colour without some trace of white. An ideal specimen will therefore have a few traces well concealed on its belly.

Above: **Long-haired Rex**
This is a Chocolate, Cream and White specimen. It has proved possible to combine the Rex coat with both smooth and long coats.

Above right: **Silver Agouti Rex**
The Rex mutation affects the hair, including the whiskers, giving rise to a woolly appearance.

Right:
Tricolour Rex and Himalayan
The original strain of British Rex guinea pigs was derived from Dutch stock, but now Rexes of many colours have been bred, as shown.

Brindle

Similarly scarce as the Tortoiseshell, this variety should have an even combination of red and black hair. Again, this is very difficult to accomplish in practice.

Bi-coloured
This form is identical to the Tortoiseshell, except that the colours must not be clear black and clear red. Such combinations as black and white are acceptable. A Tri-coloured form is also being bred; in this instance, white is added to the pattern, corresponding to the Tortoiseshell and White.

Saffron
A Self variety of recent origin, the Saffron is not yet officially standardized for show purposes. It is lemon in colour, with red eyes. Saffrons are very attractive and will almost certainly grow rapidly in popularity as more stock becomes available to enthusiasts.

New forms
Other new varieties, such as the Sable, are also being developed at present, and may become more widespread in the future. The Satin,

Right: **Saffron Argente**
The Saffron is a relatively new and striking addition to the Self group, again with red eyes. It is an appealing lemon colour and seems assured of widespread popularity.

Below: *A selection of old and new guinea pig varieties. The familiar Tortoiseshell and White (left) is shown with the newer Harlequin (centre) and Magpie (right). The Harlequin has a coat of two colours and a brindled area of overlap.*

Index to Rabbits

Page numbers in **bold** indicate major references, including accompanying photographs. Page numbers in *italics* indicate other illustrations. Text entries are shown in normal type.

Index to Guinea Pigs

Page numbers in **bold** indicate major references, including accompanying photographs. Page numbers in *italics* indicate other illustrations. Text entries are shown in normal type.

Picture Credits

Artists
Copyright of the artwork illustrations on the pages following the artists' names is the property of Salamander Books Ltd.

Graeme Campbell Design: 50-1, 52-3

Paul Davies: 18-9, 20, 25, 26-7, 30-1, 32, 36(T), 49

Seb Quigley (Linden Artists): 22

Guy Troughton: 15, 16, 50-1, 52-3

Photographs
The publishers wish to thank the following photographers and agencies who have supplied photographs for this book. The photographs have been credited by page number and position on the page: (B)Bottom, (T)Top, (C)Centre, (BL)Bottom left etc.

Ardea London: 68-9(B, J.P. Ferrero)

Marc Henrie: Half-title page, 60(B), 61(B), 66-7, 67(B), 72(T), 73(T), 79(T), 83(T), 87-113 inclusive

Ideas into Print: 21, 24, 29, 35, 42

Cyril Laubscher: Endpapers, Title page, Copyright page, 10-1, 12, 17(T), 33, 38(T), 46-7, 48-9, 51(T), 52, 54-5, 56-7, 58-9, 60-1(T), 62-3, 64-5, 67(T), 69(T), 70-1, 71(B), 72-3(B), 74-5, 76, 77(T), 78-9(B), 80, 81, 82-3(B), 84-5(T), 84(B)

Press-tige Pictures Ltd: 64-5(B), 65(B), 70(B), 77(B)

Peter W. Scott: 15, 17(B), 36(B), 40, 44

Royal Veterinary College, Laboratory Animal Science Unit: 38(B), 39

Acknowledgements
The publishers wish to thank the following for their help in preparing this book: Animal Magic Pet Shop, Virginia Bartlett, Joanna Bennett, John and Jo Beresford, Terry and Maureen Bevis, Carol Brittain, Meg Brown, Joyce Cavanagh, Anthea Dabolins, Kathleen Davies, Martin Embry, Jackie Folland, Hugh Halliday, Martin and Cheryl Highman-Smith, Cyril Jenner, Sonya and Joscelyne Kemp, Michael Kennedy, Ryan Laubscher, Ken Lettington, Terry McDonald, Colin Mantle, Stanley Maughan, Danny O'Sullivan, Betty Pearce, Sue Pearce (Topaz Stud), Mick Plose, Annette Randle, David Rea, Jacky Richardson, Eddie and Marie Salt, Margaret Snowden, Marion Stellard, Brian and Ann Warren, Whites Pet Centre, Karen Wootton, and Members of the Mid Sussex Cavy Club. Brenda Clarke (for editorial assistance), Linda Wadey (for typing the author's manuscript).

Further reading

Brown, M. *Exhibition and Pet Rabbits* Triplegate, 1982
Denham, K. *Guinea Pigs and Chinchillas* Bartholomew, 1982
Elward, M. *Encyclopedia of Guinea Pigs* TFH Publications, 1980
Haggerty, V. *Love Your Rabbit* Foulsham 1984
Henwood, C. *Love Your Guinea Pig* Foulsham, 1985
Nightingale, G. *Rabbit Keeping* Bartholomew, 1979
Robinson, D. *Encyclopedia of Pet Rabbits* TFH Publications, 1979
Robinson, R. *The Right Way to Keep Rabbits* Elliot Right Way Books, 1980
Sheail, J. *Rabbits and Their History* David and Charles, 1971
Sole, A. *Cavies* Cassell, 1975
Turner, I. *Exhibition and Pet Cavies* Spur Publications, 1977

Companion volumes of interest:

A PETKEEPER'S GUIDE TO REPTILES AND AMPHIBIANS
A PETKEEPER'S GUIDE TO HAMSTERS, GERBILS, RATS, MICE AND CHINCHILLAS
A FISHKEEPER'S GUIDE TO THE TROPICAL AQUARIUM
A FISHKEEPER'S GUIDE TO COMMUNITY FISHES
A FISHKEEPER'S GUIDE TO COLDWATER FISHES
A FISHKEEPER'S GUIDE TO MARINE FISHES
A FISHKEEPER'S GUIDE TO MAINTAINING A HEALTHY AQUARIUM
A FISHKEEPER'S GUIDE TO GARDEN PONDS
A FISHKEEPER'S GUIDE TO AQUARIUM PLANTS
A FISHKEEPER'S GUIDE TO CENTRAL AMERICAN CICHLIDS
A FISHKEEPER'S GUIDE TO FISH BREEDING
A FISHKEEPER'S GUIDE TO AFRICAN AND ASIAN CATFISHES

Sable Angora Rabbit